NASOS VAYENAS · THE ...DER

Nasos Vayenas

The Perfect Order

Selected Poems 1974–2010

Edited by
Richard Berengarten
and
Paschalis Nikolaou

Anvil Press Poetry

Published in 2010
by Anvil Press Poetry Ltd
Neptune House 70 Royal Hill London SE10 8RF
www.anvilpresspoetry.com

This book is published with financial assistance
from Arts Council England
and from the Alexander S. Onassis Foundation

Designed and set in Monotype Ehrhardt by Anvil
Printed and bound in Great Britain
by Hobbs the Printers Ltd

ISBN 978 0 85646 431 7

Contents

Selected Prose Writings

Key to Translators

Translators' initials are given in square brackets beneath each poem. For collaborative and adjusted versions, precedence is indicated by the order of initials.

RMB	Roderick Beaton
RB	Richard Berengarten
JC	John Chioles
RC	Robert Crist
AC	Alan Crosier
JD	John C. Davis
KF	Kimon Friar
MK	Margaret Kofod
PN	Paschalis Nikolaou
DR	David Ricks
JS	John Stathatos
CW	Chris Williams

Preface

THIS BOOK is the first full-length selection of Nasos Vayenas's poems to appear in English. It contains translations of poems written across a span of thirty-six years. Besides his collections in Greek, fifteen volumes by Vayenas have been published in eight European languages: evidence of the international resonance his work has already achieved. The first time a book by him was published outside Greek was in English, in 1978, nearly a decade before any such appearance in other languages. In the thirty-two intervening years between that small press edition and this present volume, many English translations of Vayenas's poems have accumulated in various versions. Sporadic publication has occurred in literary magazines, in 'special issues' on Greece, and in several anthologies of Greek literature.

In selecting and arranging the poems for this edition, we have aimed at adequate representation of each of Vayenas's volumes and attempted to balance early, middle and recent work. We have opted for chronological presentation and follow the original order of the poems in each collection. As for choosing versions, we have taken full advantage of existing material, both published and unpublished, always looking for the twin qualities necessary in all effective translation: loyalty to the source text and craftsmanship in the target language. At all stages, our editorial approach has been integrative. In representing the work of twelve translators (English, American, Australian and Greek), as well as indicating the trajectory of the poet's previous publications in English over more than three decades, this *Selected Poems* allows for a multiplicity of interpretations, timbres, voices and accents. We believe this approach particularly suits Vayenas's poetry, especially bearing in mind its variety of modes, moods and styles.

Concluding with a bibliography and notes, this volume also includes four short prose texts. In one of these Vayenas writes, 'If the translation of poetry is impossible, then the translation of poetry is a genuine art.' One might add: not only does the translation of poetry begin in impossibility, but it finds its own art through myriad possible routes, as the bonds of content and form, including inherent rhythmic and sonic effects, are sought again and again in another language and culture, and at other points in time. This is also perhaps one reason why so many poets translate – and broaden and deepen their own voices through doing so.

The taste a translation leaves on the tongue may often be bittersweet, recalling lost or at least absent presences. Similarly, in the labour of editing, just as in that of translating, there always remain ghosts of roads not taken. Even so, we hope this book succeeds in providing a valid and representative selection in English of the oeuvre and achievement of a poet who may be justly regarded as one of the leading voices of his generation in Greece.

RICHARD BERENGARTEN AND PASCHALIS NIKOLAOU

Cambridge and Corfu
April 2010

Introduction

POETRY READERS don't necessarily want introductions to such poetry as they encounter in translation; yet the duty of hospitality suggests introductions should at least be offered. The poems of Nasos Vayenas afford various points of entry: mine will be to consider their author as, *par excellence*, a poet-critic.

That might mean different things to different people, and the formulation isn't naturally such as to whet the appetite. The brief biographical sketch that follows will make clear that, yes, Vayenas is a poet-critic in the plain sense that he has written plenty of poetry and, over the same period, plenty of criticism. But poet-critics come in various guises – some of which stand self-condemned in the *dramatis personae* of our poet's collection, *Garland* (2004). Charity forbids attaching names to these types here; but we are all familiar with the lyric poet who sometimes or even habitually writes rhapsodic prose about other poets, or with the hardened critic who, shyly or with increasing bravado, supplements an uninspired critical oeuvre with equally uninspiring versifying. And, in between these two commonly found extremes, there are many poets, some of high excellence, in whom the exercise of their art and their critical discourse does not achieve an easy balance. If I mention just the case of Cavafy, whose critical pronouncements (at least in the form in which they have been transmitted to us) seem disappointingly crude compared to his poems, it will be clear that I do not see failure to be a poet-critic in this strong sense as any dishonour. Yet with Vayenas the creative and critical faculties are inseparable: in an earlier attempt to capture this, I wrote of him as being a poet 'whose verse is, in the best sense, always critical'.

The art critic Robert Hughes cunningly appropriates Iago's words for the title of his essay collection, *Nothing if not*

Critical. The phrase fits Vayenas like a glove. Just as the well-spring of his criticism is nothing other than a deep, catholic, yet austerely discriminating acquaintance with tradition (of which more below), so too the backbone of his poetry is a critical sense. This should not be confused with facile notions of cultural critique – though such a critique, often of a satisfyingly bracing kind, is by no means absent from Vayenas's work. An animus which has its root in an authentically critical outlook animates his poetry; while the poetry in turn performs one of poetry's most important functions, which is to be the most important form of criticism.

Nothing could be further from the baleful doctrine of 'the critic as artist', and Vayenas's laconic poems and slashing critical sorties build up, not just in parallel, but in interrelation. Reaching for a comparison, I can't do better for the English reader than point to Donald Davie's lifelong poetic-cum-critical enterprise, without wishing to turn this into a Seferis-style essay, 'Nasos Vayenas – Donald Davie: parallels'. Like Davie, Vayenas is acutely preoccupied with the fortunes of what we have come to call Modernism; like Davie, he understands the history and practice of translation to be, not only an integral part of poetic history, but a particularly fructifying one; like Davie, he has been as hard on himself in his own poetry as he can be on others as a critic.

Nasos Vayenas (the surname, 'Cooper', is stressed on the final syllable) was born in the town of Drama, northern Greece, not far from the Bulgarian border, in 1945. His father, who owned a timber firm, spent several years in internal exile following the Civil War (1946–1949) and with the collapse of the family enterprise moved to Athens in 1960, where he worked as a translator. The son excelled not only scholastically but on the football field, achieving selection for the national youth team; and though Vayenas has never gone as far as Frost in identifying the athlete as 'the poet's next of kin' in college, football is not only thematically present in his work ('The Perfect Order', p. 62), but has done something to colour his outlook, with its self-questioning sense of how to maintain form in the face of physical decline. Versatility has marked his positional sense throughout: posturing critics have fallen to his hard but fair tackles, while less agile poets have watched his goalmouth exploits, when a last line is perfectly slotted home, with open-mouthed admiration.

Off the field, Vayenas was acquiring a literary education which formed a capacious reservoir for the poetic decades that followed. The study of Greek literature at the University of Athens in those days (1963–1968), with all its undoubted limitations, embraced a wide historical range, from the ancient classics through the Byzantine period to the present, and Vayenas's work has in common with the best poets of his generation the natural recourse to such material which in younger hands can seem mannered. Again, some of his early scholarly publications are marked by the sober literary-historical knowledge which most poets, with their whimsically chosen elective affinities, have never taken the trouble to possess. Yet Vayenas has also noted more recently how the influence of one of his teachers in particular, the poet Kostas Stergiopoulos, came as a breath of fresh air; and it is perhaps in part owing to the older man's sympathies that Vayenas has sought to rehabilitate minor, even lost, figures of the poetic past (see, for a key example, 'Interior Monologue of Stephanos Martzokis', p. 97).

By the time Vayenas graduated, Greece had succumbed to the Colonels' philistine and bullying régime (1967–1974), and on completing national service in the navy he must have been glad to follow a traditional path of the Athenian philology graduate by going to Rome for further study (1970–1972). From the Cretan Renaissance to the recent past, the influence of Italian poetry on Greek poetry has been central, and Vayenas has been concerned not least with the poets in this intellectual line – notably the two founding poets of the modern tradition, Count Dionysios Solomos and Andreas Calvos (see e.g. 'Calvos in Geneva', p. 57), whose poetic oeuvre in each case spanned the two languages.

The final part of Vayenas's literary apprenticeship, at least as marked by formal education, was a prolonged stay in England (1972–1979). This began with an MA in literary translation at the University of Essex, by then lacking Donald Davie, but still hospitable to literary study beyond national boundaries: here Vayenas wrote a dissertation on Borges. ('Jorge Luis Borges in University Street', p. 67, records a real incident, and Vayenas saw the old master made an honorary doctor of the University of Crete in 1984.) This was followed in due course by enrolment at King's College, Cambridge, the alma mater of Greek poetry's most charismatic advocate in those years, the late G. P. Savidis. Cambridge was also where Vayenas met his first translator (and co-editor of this volume), Richard Berengarten (Burns).

Vayenas's doctoral thesis on the Nobel Laureate George Seferis, *The Poet and the Dancer*, had on its publication in Greek (1979) the unusual and deserved distinction of becoming a best-seller. This closely argued work, based on a wealth of documentation, is unlikely to be superseded. Among its particular critical virtues are its close attention to Seferis's poetic formation in the round, acknowledging not just his French and English influences (on which, unsurprisingly, many had had much to say, pro and contra), but also on Seferis's roots in the modern Greek tradition. This meant going beyond Seferis's own cautious but clear declaration of a debt to C. P. Cavafy and extending the discussion to the even now unfashionable Angelos Sikelianos, a largely unacknowledged but deeper influence. In going against the critical grain, but without the impassioned rhetoric of someone who wants to be watched righting a wrong, Vayenas was also quietly adumbrating a poetic programme, with close but never adulatory attention to Sikelianos in the following years.

In the meantime, Vayenas had made an equally strong poetic début with *Field of Mars* (1974). (He is said to have disowned an earlier collection from undergraduate years.) This book came out in the final year of the Junta, and its title (the *Pedion Areos*, 'Champs de Mars', is an Athenian park) is of course coloured by the sanguinary history his country had lived through, with the violent suppression of the Polytechnic in 1973 in particular. The selection in the present volume perhaps tilts away from poems in which politics more clearly casts its shadow; but, even allowing for this, it is clear that Vayenas's poetic response to his times is both strikingly mature and relatively reticent. Yet, though rightly inclined to mock such labels as a general rule, Vayenas has never sought to disavow his origins in the highly talented 'Generation of the Seventies', and he shares with Jenny Mastoraki and Michalis Ganas their precocity, their deep recourse to tradition, and their terseness. The first of these qualities was early noted by Vayenas's critics; the second is, as we shall see, ever-present; and the last is testified to by the short length of most of Vayenas's verse collections, as of all the poems that make them up, and by the fact that they even now form a corpus modest by Greek standards. (It is worth noting that the poet has yet to publish a collected or selected poems.) Vayenas's realistic expectations of himself – likewise his suspicion of those who fail to hold themselves to such standards – is clear from 'Apologia', the poem with which this selection begins (p. 27).

Books of poetry have followed since in a stream represented faithfully in the present volume: *Biography* (1976), *Roxane's Knees* (1981), *Travels of a Stay-at-Home* (1986), *Flyer's Fall* (1989), *Barbarous Odes* (1992), *Flyer's Fall, II* (1997), *Dark Ballades and Other Poems* (2001), the National Prize-winning *Garland* (2004) and *On the Isle of the Blest* (2010). There have been changes of emphasis and experiments with different techniques, but never a sense that

Vayenas is just fighting the last war or lumbering from one fashion to the next. This is poetry marked by circumspection, a cultivatedly ironic perspective, and serious but not sombre self-examination.

These latter qualities could hardly be absent given the stringency of Vayenas's own critical judgements and his apprenticeship in Borges, whose text on Shakespeare, 'Everything and Nothing', has made a great impression on him. In that book of his which has come closest to cult status, *The Guild* (1976), Vayenas presented some Borgesian fables of his own, as also in *The Labyrinth of Silence* (1982). Among his creations in *The Guild* were the poet Patroclus Yiatras, the putative author of the mordant epitaphs which make up *Garland*. A preoccupation with the masters of irony – which in the Greek twentieth century means, above all, Cavafy and the elegist, satirist, and suicide K. G. Karyotakis (1896–1928) – marks Vayenas's criticism and poetry alike; but he has been keen to resist the idea that this makes him a Post-Modernist *malgré lui*. Instead, irony is used, as it is with Cavafy, in the service of a historical sense. Woe betide the critic who opines complacently about the naivety of past Greek writers or critics: setting the historical record straight – notably when it comes to modern Greek literature's longstanding and fertile transactions with European poetry – has been Vayenas's constant concern. Over his long teaching career, first at the newly founded University of Crete (1980–1991), where he was able to shape an ambitious literature curriculum, and since then at the University of Athens (where his chair is, as it happens, not in literature but Literary Theory and Criticism), he has sought to broaden sympathies but also (in the service of the same cause) to clip the wings of the vatic or the merely vain.

This might make Vayenas sound like the advocate of a Little Hellas in ways that recall the more unimaginative sides of the Movement in England. As with Donald Davie, however – I invoke him once again – this would clearly be a distortion. Let me take up two aspects which show Vayenas both at his most critical and at his most acute when it comes to making his own poems.

The first is his preoccupation with verse translation, which makes him (though of course his translations cannot be represented here) an unusually appropriate candidate *for* translation. Contemporary Greek letters present an odd picture here: the literary culture combines a great (and perhaps increasing) dependency on translation, combined with a remarkable lack of attention to translation as a part of living literature or even of the literary past. Vayenas has fought a long critical battle on behalf of translation, notably in the lucid book, *Poetry and Translation* (1989, expanded edition 2004). Translation has been integral to his poetry. Particularly in the two *Flyer's Fall* volumes, where translated poems are – very unusually for a Greek poet – interspersed with his own, we find, both the development of multiple personas (how else would Berryman and Williams, Calvino and Zanzotto and others find themselves bedfellows?), and the accumulation of a personal idiom versatile enough to embrace them all. A poet who holds, with Vayenas, that 'No poem is a real poem unless it possesses the character of the poet's spoken discourse', is setting the bar high for the translator who (again, with Vayenas) understands a translation to be a new poem; and among Vayenas's most unflinching critical judgements has been his dethroning of Seferis's standard translation of *The Waste Land*. Vayenas himself does more as a verse translator than simply 'do the police in different voices': to be translated by him (I can attest) is to admire the adroitness of his choices and his inventiveness of his re-forming of a poem.

The unusual centrality of translation in Vayenas's work needs emphasizing for a congeries of reasons. First, as I have noted, he understands one of the distinctions of modern

Greek poetry over the years to have been its embrace of translation, and indeed its creation of genres which are at the limits between translation and 'original'. In this, of course, he is faithful to the poetic of Pound and Eliot, and perhaps above all of Eliot's essay on *Homage to Sextus Propertius*. But he has also sought to prevent translation's being hived off as a parergon of the poet. For Vayenas translation is (as we see by implication in 'Torment', p. 28) a mirror to hold up against the poet, a salutary reminder that his medium is words.

A last, and perhaps the most important, motive for Vayenas's emphasis on translation is his sense that the poets form a guild which transcends languages – not just as a matter of historical fact, but as an aspiration, albeit an aspiration constantly called into question by the resistances of language. His poem titles alone display a wide range of names, but I should emphasize that this amounts to more than the name-dropping rolodex employed by so many poets. (With Auden, say, this was a clear sign that he was off his game; and many Greek poets are equally prodigal with dedications designed to impress.) Vayenas sets out to weave other poets into his work through his finding of himself in and through their words. An exhaustive catalogue of evidence is of course both unattainable – it would require Vayenas's breadth of reading – and out of place here; but a few pointers to the present selection may give the English reader a sense of what is at stake here.

The tone is set by the echo in the opening poem selected, 'Apologia', with its self-reflexive echo of Cavafy's quasi-autobiographical 'Byzantine Nobleman, In Exile, Versifying'. But we can then go on to identify several types of enlistment. The most obvious kind, of course, is when a poet is actually named in the title or text: 'Jorge Luis Borges in University Street' (along with Homer and Solomos in the body of the poem, p. 67) is a ready example; likewise 'Calvos in Geneva' (again with internal references to Alfieri and

Foscolo, p. 57) or 'Lord Byron in Rethymno' (p. 65). Other named presences, even before we reach the named sonnets that comprise *On the Isle of the Blest* (2010), embrace Cavafy and Seferis, Rimbaud, Brecht, and Dante. Beyond this, there are clear allusions to other poets ancient and modern: Eliot ('The Performance, II', p. 30) and Yeats ('The Second Coming', p. 98); Horace ('Barbarous Odes, XVI', p. 83) – along with more speculatively established connections to poets from Donne to Geoffrey Hill. Above all, of course, we have shades cast over whole collections, whether these be individuals or a 'familiar compound ghost'. *Flyer's Fall* (likewise its paradoxically named successor *Flyer's Fall, II*) takes its cue from Stevens (whose poem with that title does indeed appear in the first book); *Barbarous Odes* likewise are a tribute to Carducci's *Odi barbare*; and over *Dark Ballades* falls the shadow of a minor *poète maudit*, Stephanos Martzokis. Finally, *Garland* recalls the *Garland* of Meleager, Cavafy's neo-Alexandrian 'tomb' poems, and the exactly contemporary *Spoon River Anthology*.

But it's worth emphasizing at the same time that, despite Vayenas's critical attention to the tradition – and he is as ruthless in separating the wheat from the chaff as Davie ever was, with the same insistence on disciplined expression – he is generally as reticent in voicing his poetic loves as he is self-ironizing in the use of (as they might seem) autobiographical themes. It has taken the acutest of critics to discern, for example, that Sikelianos has such importance for Vayenas's poetry: motifs from the unbridled lyrical mysticism of the older poet generally appear in cunningly transmuted, and indeed muted, form. Likewise, Vayenas's debt to the two most powerful post-war Greek poets, Takis Sinopoulos and Manolis Anagnostakis, is evident only in subtle details of form or glancing hints. As an ironist *par excellence*, it has been Vayenas's stance to stand aside from the -isms incautiously embraced by others. His abiding poetic affinity for the distinctive and precious tradition of the Ionian Islands, of which Sikelianos was the last representative, is indicative of this.

One way of capturing this stance is to emphasize what one critic has seen as Vayenas's preoccupying theme: the moon. In a poetic culture obsessed with light (and the word *phōs* derives part of its resonance from being one of only a handful of monosyllables in the language) Vayenas has consistently turned, not to the sun which Greek poets can often regard as their national property, but to the moon. This most lunar of poets responds to that heavenly body which shines *notho lumine*, in the expression of one of Vayenas's earliest poetic idols, Catullus. This borrowed, spurious, literally 'bastard' light for Vayenas comes from the words of other poets as reflected in his own: he is always conscious that what he takes from them at once is and is not rightfully his.

The qualities of irony and reticence that govern Vayenas's poetic forms are fairly represented in this selection and call for only brief comment. Through all the various formal manoeuvres he has carried out through the years – and readers will have their preferences among them – an allegiance to short, circumspect sentences thickly punctuated remains a constant; so too a nostalgia for and at the same time renunciation of the singing line – in this, he is a true successor to Anagnostakis. Vayenas has pleaded, against the card-carrying Post-Modernists, for the 're-enchantment of poetic discourse', but he does not understand by that the reproduction furniture of New Formalism. (Instead, the English reader coming to him as part of Anvil's distinguished list may find in Donald Justice more of a kindred spirit, and not only because both poets are avowed heirs of Stevens.) Rather, let me cite one of Vayenas's truest and most trenchant critical formulations, one to which he has made his own poems true: 'Sikelianos shows us, better than any other modern Greek poet, that the distinction between traditional and modern is without meaning.'

I have tried here to identify what I see as some key features of Nasos Vayenas's poetry, features which may help to open up that poetry to an English reader. But the poems that follow can speak for themselves, and may indeed speak against some of my observations. In seeking to pay tribute to this most critical of poets, I can't help being brought up short by the shortest of the poems in *Garland*, 'Elias Kagios'. That stark reminder of the fate of critics as of poets goes simply like this: 'I entered the gates of Hades trembling / lest even here I come in for praise from Nezeritis.'

DAVID RICKS

The Poems

Apologia

Regardless of events I've not changed my convictions.
I remain the same with the same ideas
that pierce into my brain like thorns. It's
things around me that keep changing.
The heights of buildings. The prices of cars.
The opinions of my friends. I remain the same person
with ideas that have scarred me indelibly
with ideas that walk around in my skull like ants.
It's probably from this that the prosaic quality
of my verses derives. The evident
lack of lyrical exaltation.
Which makes so many of my friends
look at me with pity
like a lost cause
like an unfulfilled promise.

[KF & RB]

Torment

Wrong again in my metaphors.
Words elude me. Like betrayers
they tumble, like pieces of silver.
My lines give me away.
They have a will of their own.
They distort my personal vision.
They brazenly conjure decadent poets.

And yet the first words came out right.
The first line was quite perfect
in getting the feelings across.
But too soon
it got contaminated
by the memory of some
awful foreign poems.

[RB & PN]

The Performance

It was time for you to go on. But you didn't.
You weren't even in the theatre. You stayed at home
looking at the trees from your window. Or turning
bored onto your other side
before falling asleep.

And the others just watching in silence.
Wondering what's going on. Looking at each other
in despair when the conspicuous gaps occur.
The unexpected silences and pauses.

[MK]

The Performance, II

even though you are
a minor character in the play.
One of those who open a scene. Who stand by
the hero at the hour of the duel. Who attend
the king. Or who disappear in the first act.
But they remain hidden behind the scenes
(where stagehands and electricians
indifferently play cards).
Watching secretly from the curtains
while the bodies drop one by one.
Waiting for the moment to go on
when everyone has forgotten them
when no-one expects them any more.

[MK]

Death in Exarchia

They told me you were dead. And now I find you
in the café playing backgammon with the living.
Even winning. And wearing a tie.
You never wore a tie.
You never went to the square.
You always shut yourself up in that house
silently watching the neighbours and passers-by.

They told me you were dead. Who should I believe?
You vanished suddenly without saying a word.
Without even leaving a note.
Your shutters were closed. Your bell broken.
The dog broken-hearted. And the lights out.

Is it you? Or not? Who should I believe?
How your voice has changed.
The others say nothing. They watch you play.
They watch you throwing the dice and smiling.
And winning all the time. All the time.

You never won. You were always the loser.

[MK]

Death will come . . .

Death will come and take me by surprise.
This death that keeps me company
from morning till night.
That hides in my clothes and my hair.
That appears like a sudden stain on my shirt.
That sticks like a crumb to the palate.
That keeps crawling over this skin
like a slight shudder.

You'll go on sleeping regardless. But your
breasts will stand terrified in the darkness.
They'll listen out for the footsteps on the stairs.
For the door creak. All night
they'll watch the shadows at the window.

I shan't even have finished this poem.

[KF & RB]

The Wake

When will you stop it.
You come back every evening
in your bitter mask
in your black dress.
You sit on the bed and say nothing.
And you adorn me
with red flowers
with lit candles.
Hang golden oil lamps from the ceiling.
Bend down and kiss me for the last time.

You leave only when the neighbours wake.

[PN & RB]

A Game of Chess

How can I beat you. You do
what you want with me. And you take
my pawns one by one. You surround
my castles. You've terrified my knights
and they stagger around in confusion.

But how can I beat you. When even
this queen of mine sneaks off.
And betrays me shamelessly on the grass
with your soldiers and your officers.

[KF & RB]

Saturday

It's warm tonight. The Americans
are wearing nylon raincoats. Outside the museum
the coaches are snarled up and the traffic warden's shouting.
That cloud is like cotton wool on the wound. As dusk
    descends
the birds in the trees light up one by one.

In the trees the birds light up one by one.

                                    [JS]

Episode

All night long it rained. And in the morning
the trucks descended with muddy tyres.
The dead move into other bodies leaving
large scratches on the skin.
The sky quickly
turns blue.
A scorching sun passes
whistling above my head.
'There's nothing to death,' a taxi
driver was telling me the other day.
'Simply, the light's been cut off. As when
you can't pay your bill.'

[KF]

Eden

Warm wind of autumn was coming
in among the leaves.
Or rather, it was spring because
the sun had not set yet.

I couldn't make up my mind.
You couldn't make up your mind.
A tramp stretched on the grass kept turning
now into an angel
now into a snake.

Above us the apple
had started rotting.

[RB]

from Biography

II

Darkness is creeping over me. A plant. Which you
    water in secret every morning.

It's your breath too. It shuts me away from every-
    where like barbed wire. Under your skin

Lie seven cities. One beneath the other. Endlessly
    circling

The walls of each a chariot drags the glorious dead.

III

In a blue bus. At seventy miles per hour. Under a
    scorching sky.

Among forty sweaty people. Who smoke. Dream. Or
    eat sandwiches.

And a middle aged driver with a handkerchief over
    his neck. Who now and then spits out of the
    window. And keeps putting on

Cassettes of old songs . . .

All songs will be forgotten. The bus will be scrap.
    The people earth.

The dark skinned man with the sideburns and light
    blue shirt sitting next to me says he is going to
    Katerini.

V

Here I am again in darkness. Naked. My love spread
all over my body.

I embrace you. I leave for the skies. I float in outer
space.

You stay on earth. Burning holes in your shoes.
They stick to the pavement. A damp forest

Crosses your body diagonally.

At night I am awoken by the grass that grows on
your skin.

VI

With my head stuffed with unwritten poems I look
    up at the stars.

The stars. A figure of speech. Heaven does not exist.

Uprooted angels are on the prowl on earth. Out of
    work. And with short back and sides.

(That tall bloke in the dole queue. His wings are
    tucked under his shirt.)

When night falls they go down to the taverns. Get
    pissed. And spit and curse.

IX

30 September 1970. In a plush seated compartment I
read

Of Alexander Kerensky's death at Berkeley in the
United States.

I didn't know he was alive. It had never even crossed
my mind. Half a century away from the Winter
Palace . . . O dark train.

You are not Lenin's train but the Salonika-Athens
inter-city service.

Which will never arrive at St Petersburg. And I

Without flags. Without leaflets. My suitcase packed
with coloured brochures. Not an

Implacable commissar. Or secretary of a local
committee.

But travelling representative for a cosmetics
company.

With flair. Imagination. A sound grasp of the
market. With excellent prospects of promotion.

XI

Why go any further? Since the landscape will be no
different.

Deep skies. Covered with blue. Below them the
green creeps onward. The trees

Put out their blossoms in a way I can't understand.

Trucks go by. The man sitting beside me keeps
agreeing and disagreeing with himself.

My senses glide out of my skin. A beautiful woman

Her body suddenly darkens. Like a photo over-
exposed.

XVI

Like a man who arrives breathless at the post office
with an urgent letter. And the post office has just
closed.

Like a man who sets foot in a foreign land for the
first time. And doesn't know a word of the
language.

I stand rooted on the steps of Syntagma Square.
With my voice stuck in my throat.

Foreign banks. Vending machines. Department stores.
Neon lights flashing

Over sweaty faces and all convictions scrambled.

Eunuchs sing the Internationale. An insignificant
librettist

Is proclaimed poet. And those who were once first to
whip the tradesmen from the temple

Now with their very own stalls in the central
precinct . . .

With my collar up I cross over into the last quarter of
the century.

XVII

The ground is rising. It keeps on rising. It's covering
  you.

You do nothing about it. You're waiting for rain. To
  put out new shoots. So you say. But don't really
  believe it.

If there were birds there would also be branches. If
  there were branches you would be one too.

Not the highest one of course. But strong enough
  for someone to find a foothold.

XIX

Oh my country. Country betrayed. Who would have
  believed it. That I should be sitting here writing
  patriotic poems.

Under deep-set boarded windows the voices of the
  living cry out.

The dead awaken. They put on their shoes and arise

On wide-lit escalators silently weeping.

Weeping they scale the streetlamps. They unscrew
  the bulbs.

Massive slabs of glory float through the dark.

[RB]

Déjeuner sur l'Herbe

Pigeons strut up and down a parched lawn. Right
next to your body. I take

photographs. The camera records the mortal side of
you.

(The lake in the background. A wooden bridge. The
stilled ducks. Lilies on the water.)

It starts drizzling. The rain brings forgotten crevices
to light.

Further off a woman tries to escape. Trapped in a net
of wrinkles.

[RB]

Roxane's Knees

It's hardly an essential component of eternal truth that you should wear high mauve heels tipped with little gold rings. Or that you should strive to pull out your most gorgeous limbs from the very teeth of time. Green leaves clatter down, covering the earth. There are more things to be seen on the ground than could ever be imagined. It occurs to me: if death does exist, it's mainly because of his longing to over-turn the natural order of things. Give me your hand. Time isn't a liar and out of all the things he passes judgement on, perhaps something may get left

on your skin, some tiny snippet of immortality.

[RB & PN]

The Birth of Aphrodite

Some day I will set you inside a seashell.
On a white cloud pulled by doves.
I will dress you in red veils. With flowers.
The wind will blow softly.

Or I will place you inside
a forest with the fragrance of apples.
At a window with green leaves
and far-off a blue river.
(Above you, winged Eros in flight.)

Botticelli must have felt a similar need
when he got his wife to model for him.
At the moment when everything was over.
Just before their separation.

[JC]

Ode

No matter how much iron and concrete you build
    with, deep down you're still a Turkish hovel.

The years fall upon you, sending up a cloud of dust.
    Through which History passes, coughing.

Why is your snow as heavy as marble? Why do the
    pigeons that peck your grass fly away keening?

You're an LP playing at 78. A blue bus with one
    wheel stuck in the mud.

Greece, what fingers are poking down your throat?
    Bending over me you vomit blood and eternity.

[MK]

Sostenuto

Reach out and touch the sky.
Wipe the dusty stars clean. Climb
the highest branch. Warble.
Hide the whole town behind your hand.
Paint darkness green. Or orange.
Drink the water in the sea down to the last drop.
Bend life the way village strongmen
bent iron bars at fairgrounds.
Take everything back to the word go – start off with
    clay and mud.
Cross the same river twice.
Turn iron to fire. Snow to stone.
Tell me nothing's impossible.
Tell me nothing's impossible.

[PN & RB]

Incas

Ash on the skin.
And a candle in the pocket
for the darkness in your voice.
Once there was a time when there
was no America. That time is gone.

As is gone
the time of our passions.
Since the first ships
arrived.

[PN & RB]

Orpheus in the Overworld

They laid out branches in front of the windows. Planted the necessary trees. But houses also have sewers. Thin horizontal pipes like veins carry the day's effluent to the underworld.

Of such materials is life made. Of such pipes is life built. And yet, if you follow their notional extensions – who knows – you might some day meet with Eurydice.

[JS]

Clean Curtains

Loves I allow and passions I approve:
A warm cup of coffee in the morning.
Reading the paper (the slower, the better).
Some rain, now and again, to bathe the emotions.
The soil on your new high heels.
Sea in the afternoon with a bit of cloud.
Carnations. Lots of carnations.

In addition:
Chagall's 'Man leaping over the city'.
Going up old wooden stairs.
My hand on your breast.
Certain Cavafy poems.

But mostly, my hand on your breast.

[PN]

National Garden

As if it were some scene arranged by
a great European director in a moment of inspiration

and not by the light passing over the trees
slowly shifting the shadows towards the avenue.

The whole image had something of the atmosphere
of certain Renaissance paintings.

And if it weren't for that man on the bench
his head in his hands

and that woman vomiting two steps further on
it would be perfect: a picture-postcard you send

from a country you've just arrived in
with a couple of words about the weather, the people – general
    first impressions

from a journey you've planned for years
when everything turns out as you'd imagined.

[CW]

Beautiful Summer Morning

(an unfinished painting)

Beautiful morning. Full of light.
A gentle breeze is blowing.

The superb sun of Attica.
Deep blue. White birds.

Beneath, warm
chairs on the sand.
And, naturally, the sea.

Nonetheless, it could use a few trees.
And one or two boats on the sea. To show

that one's able
to depart.

[CW]

Calvos in Geneva

An old settee. A creaking chair.
Curtains closed. The table narrow.

Tragedies by Alfieri on the shelf.
And enraged letters from Foscolo.

Winter. Cold air. Rain. The river.
(On whose other side Count Capo d'Istria

posts letters to St Petersburg.
And waits. And waits. And waits.)

At night, he either walks in a heavy coat
through real and non-existent streets:

Grand' Rue. Place St Germais. Rue Beauregard.
Freedom Street. *Rue du Soleil-Levant.* Virtue Street –

or somehow he writes in broken Greek
on paper borrowed from the *Société de Lecture.*

[CW]

Notes

The moon goddess be praised. For years on end I
    dyed her high heels. And she hasn't forgotten
    me.

Last night, just before I fell asleep something glis-
    tened on my skin: a hint of evergreen.

And cool air on my forehead. As if through a broken
    window.

[PN & RB]

A Way of Looking at the Sky

My sorrow – a whole weekend away in the country –
  has come back with her face suntanned.

Here's a theme: 'The influence of ultraviolet rays on
  the formation of the consciousness of infinity'.

More precisely: when the gold teeth of dawn
  gleam . . .

But the light is mostly your pale hands. That stand
  out – like Mycenae – from death.

[RB & PN]

Interior Monologue of Georgios Hortatzis

The trees all move towards the forest
into which richer entity each blends.
The forest moves towards the other forest.
To Pasiphaë the bull descends.

By science are nature's errors rectified.
Penalties get booted by the best shot.
Prows not sterns are made to slice the tide
and Eros through our whole lot.

[RB & PN]

Old Song

You change the new day into to an old one by
    shuffling some of morning's colours around.
    Then there is the wind. It blows hard, shifting
    details. It opens out folds of truth I'd never have
    imagined. E.g. that your eyes are made of stone.

I touch your breasts. Against a smooth backdrop of
    green sea

they're like dark dice. Cast centuries ago.

[RB & PN]

The Perfect Order

The poppy's quiet bombast enthrals me.

So does the rope-ladder of the preacher's voice on
   Sunday.

And also: the sound of evening rain on the inky
   membranes of November.

As in a dream I watch the fans going crazy. At the
   precise moment when the PAOK–Panathinaikos
   match is drawn. (A corking header from
   Terzanides in the 90th minute.)

The brilliant birds. The slippery slope in Veria. The
   armchair near the radiator. Carnations . . .

Warm curve of the moon: you are irreplaceable.

Death: you are light's silken lining.

[MK & RB]

Theme in White

Icy century. (This is the hour when dawn spreads
   mystic in Sumatra.) Endless drizzle.

Time's watery edges. And this racket they call
   music.

Leaves scurry across the ground like mice. In and
   out

of that deep warm green dream I keep seeing.

[RB & PN]

Pisces

White sky. Milk overflowing. Where you take your
   bath laughing loudly. Like a Roman empress.

In other words, a delicate surplus of nothingness.
   Over which you glide like a maniac. Whirling

in rusty ice skates. On the TV screen right now – a
   herd of terrified reindeer.

'The music that inhabits me is the irrefutable proof
   of truth,'

said a wise man. Some people believed him.

(When I consider myself in relation to the
   universe ... etc.)

Strokings plus other tactile achievements. Dark
   kisses. Velvet carnations. Your hair

a thousand weary birds covering my face.

All night I kept trying to cross the lines of a palm.

[PN & RB]

64

Lord Byron in Rethymno

I've come to you late. Too late, Rethymno. With
your dusty sea and futile minarets.

Now I'm trying to unwind your streets from a
tangled ball of string.

From your sky some old ropes dangle.
Disintegrating.

And all your houses have deserted me.

[PN & RB]

Love Games

I

Like a Hindu nun. With the merest hint of a thought, you fill infinity.

Which slips in deep through my veins. And dislodges everything.

Eros plays billiards with my corpuscles. A cigarette stuck between his lips.

II

The Himalayas are the laughter of Shiva. Just as the wind is the vowels of your name.

Wind, unceasing.

Rethymno's red moons tumble at my feet. Softly flows the dark. (Almost tenderly, I'd say.)

[PN & RB]

Jorge Luis Borges in University Street

Survivor of your own death
clutching at a deflated Attic sun
slowly you walk up University Street
with a slim walking stick. Chesterton's.

Borges – blind.
Polyphemus.
Your voice sends sap through my bones.
Deep down, you're a Greek.
The light has sat astride your shoulders.
                                        Beneath
ink-black eyelids you make out
Solomos, a tipsy shadow.
You're pursued by Homer – in a black cab.
Out on the town all night.
Bedraggled, dishevelled.
He stubs out one cigarette after another.
And collects the coin
that now and then
tumbles from your gleaming teeth.

3 September 1983

[RB & PN]

Dolce Stil Novo

I hear the hiss and whirling of time's bomb.
But nowhere does a plane show in the sky.
The bomb no doubt will go off when I die
but maybe with no great resounding boom

of any kind. For if my fortune crests,
with the right handling the whole scheme of things
might change – as if levitated by strings
invisibly attached to the pert breasts

of some sweet goddess who, but half-awake
(in her celestial garden), slowly stands
resplendent in a semi-see-through shawl

or, stooping to cool waters, with fair hands
(wearing absolutely nothing at all)
rinses white shoulders, hair and nape of neck.

[RB & PN]

The Rose Meadow

Night in another layout. With crimson moons. That
lie low. That lean against the earth.

And a strong smell of herbs. Or like an old – an age
old – olive grove on fire.

Somewhere secret guitars jangle. And the dawn is
always late.

The clothes I was wearing were ripped by an unseen
rosebush.

[PN & RB]

Hymn (or Ode perhaps)

to the moon. To most stars. To tenderest
September.

To the large globules of night. That drip slowly
on my head.

To the sea at Rethymno. To Arthur Rimbaud
('Devotion').

I gazed long hours into the blue mirror, the corroded
face of eternity.

To the ruins of Philippoi.

To X. Unknown.

To Seferis's line: 'and then the smiles, so static, of
the statues'. To the splendid curve of a high
note from the throat of a famous Italian soprano.

To Anna – and down I sank within your deep hair.
Hotel Volturno, via degli Apuli 44.

I discover splendour at the memory of an
impromptu speech delivered under a tree during
a land allocation project by Nikolaos Tepetzi-
kiotis, Prefect of Grevena.

To the line of clothes on the terrace.

To the women of the Old Masters (actual and imagi-
nary).

To those in general lost, forsaken, betrayed. To
   certain unspecified assassins. To the beautiful
   student wearing mauve

opal earrings. (Luminous I ventured forth into the
   night. Without sinking. Upon the face of the
   deep.)

To summer's open windows. To your dark hands.
   To the violet

tint of your eyes when the sky is clouded. Or when a
   strong wind blows. Or when . . .

To death . . . And springtime is the letter that I write
   you.

To Bertolt Brecht.

[RB & PN]

Anyone could see . . .

Anyone could see
his face in your face.
Even in this light.

(I wonder why I've no wings.
That is to say: even though
I've been losing my arms
I'm still in one piece.)

One by one the leaves
covering the ground
return to the branches.

[RB & PN]

Haiku

You've died. Your
blood doesn't know it yet.
Nor does your mouth.

What your shoulders
and hair gave me
I've lost.

Your glowing nails.
Irreplaceable.
Your knees. Lips.

(And once this
hand stroked
those knees.)

Not a single line
to do with love
will be left of us.

[RB & PN]

Spinoza

Baruch Spinoza, lens-grinder of Amsterdam
kept hidden within him a loud tam-tam.

In a cold dark cellar, all alone
he drummed out his morse in a constant drone

to the sky. Like Africans in the virgin bush.
Little by little he managed to push

towards the Whole. To the One. To Infinity.
Whence he spied out the nature of humanity.

(In avid thirst for Primary Causation
he almost expired from acute starvation.)

At night in his dreams lens-grinder Spinoza
slept in the arms of a certain Rosa.

Rosa Raczewski née Vamprotten.
No-one knows how they met or got on

to each other. A true blonde of genuine stock
and high-class lady. So things went tick-tock.

[MK & RB]

Wheel of Fortune

It's not what you say.
It's what you don't say
that matters. As

a forest next to a fire
makes the fire less
of a fire. Or as

your breasts break
the abyss to bits.

Trees are not
only trees. And each day
the sun makes you darker.

Slabs of earth float
through the sky. One small
puff and the world blows out.

[RB & PN]

Haiku

Awful wind.
Tree shadows are
broken umbrellas.

I take notes
from leaves and ripe
fruit falling.

[RB & PN]

from Barbarous Odes

II

Here I am once more on the edge of reality
forty kilometres from Rethymno
ankles in the Libyan Sea.
I turn from side to side

among steaming rocks
pitilessly grinding the sun.
I touch your hair which weaves
the white darkness

of day. (The anemones,
successive grave objections
to eternity, are cast aside
every now and then.)

I touch your breast which holds sway
over the sea. Your dark
body constitutes an integral
part of the truth.

[DR]

VII

Oh you who warm the chilly winter air
with your face.
You whose single (wise) book
is deepest darkness.

Roses billow in your footsteps.
Death watches you mesmerized.
Acacias shed stars. And with white meanings
blanket canvases of trucks.

Eternal mother with your golden locks
and your girlish breasts untrammelled.
How is it you offer your purple nipples
to the first passerby?

[RB & PN]

X

. . . and adoration of uplifted heads
ROMOS FILYRAS

Hot moon, boundless revolution, mother of darkness
parked on a cold edge of November.
You who make lovers dizzy beneath the trees
beneath dark foliage you
inflame them with wild passion.

And the things you light: windows, wounds, hanged men
caravans, treacheries, stationary trucks
mournful women, skies, oleanders
and everything that is born at night
and everything that dies with morning.

Solitary, proud, infallible, incorruptible, accursed,
immaculate, inscrutable, unbegun, harmonious.
I am precisely what you are within me.
I am your beloved on this planet.
I follow you naked.

I know you haven't said your last word.
I know there is nothing deeper than you.
Vigilant you watch over the quality of night.
Absorbing all sorrows. Expiating
all sins.

Prehistoric, precosmic, precataclysmic,
many-wiled, all-embracing, almighty, everlasting.
Syllable of the untold, nipple of nothingness, chimera.
Above all you are the sound of your name.
You are the visible side of nothing.

[MK]

XI

Night spreads out on the farther side of night.
Farther than your glimmering white breast.
And masses of darkness
are still left over for morning.

[RB & PN]

XIII

My old loves. Visible
hours of a century that doesn't want to die.
Moons keep breaking around me.
The light that lights me is sure to come
from long spent stars.

All night I uproot feelings from my chest
but they'll always stay green there.
Dry grass with roots in eternity.
I am dizzied by the clamour of time.
I descend

into a night even deeper than the real one.
In its corners darkness lies doubled
with mists of past eras.
I walk slowly, carefully
so as not to wake you.

[MK]

XVI

The thirst for heaven is something I don't understand.
And no, my brow has never touched the stars.
As for azaleas (what kind of word is that)
they don't do anything for me.

A cloud from 1978 drifts past.
A strong wind is blowing in from
the future. Once upon a time night
was mother of the universe. Now

she's a grey rag hanging out
in some sleazy corner of Attica. What
I keep seeing in mirrors is an unpolished
translation of myself.

A dream: gently, blue burial urns
tumble into my chest. In the lap of time
half-naked, curls a curvy blonde
plucking petals from a black daisy.

[RB & PN]

XVIII

Who could ever escape from the moon?
My skin is covered in moondust.
Night keeps whispering in my ear
cheap words of love.

And that strange plant the sun
is a parody of truth,
dragging itself thirstily all day long
over the sandhills of your breasts.

Sum of light, when will you ever
stop deducting my blood? When
will you stop throwing me
like some morsel to passing moments?

[MK & RB]

XIX

Naked woman with your deep blue-green eyes
who cleanse your flesh of darkness.
You're sinking into a sponge of music.
Hardly surprising. I'm no Vivaldi.

What was it you were saying to make the sun
bow low? This evening, night will not
fall like night. Fate's waterlogged and sinking.
Dark woman

once I was a wizard in these woods.
A sculptor of the absolute. With velvety
fingers that gently chiselled out
your knees.

[RB & PN]

XXII

The dream again: at day edge I stand
parsing the moon's rhetoric.
She, indomitable, unruffled, austere,
delivers speeches to dusk.

Roses are softly falling. Like
snippets of immortality.
Or is it the unbearable
scent of darkness dizzies me?

O night. Now the wind
blows, tossing into the air
thousands of leaves. Green,
red, yellow, black.

[RB]

XXIII

This evening your body is part of the weather.
Am I touching the clouds or your hair?
You've been falling since dawn
like thick snow.

[RC]

XXV

Fate's pale carriers, your hands
noiselessly move across the afternoon.
They sink into a frayed green.
I watch them

(auditor well-versed in the absolute)
as I calculate burnt light.
Balancing the cost of spring
with the weights of winter.

[RB & PN]

XXVI

Going down cracked steps
having just escaped from the blue
by staining the lace of twilight
with the oil of truth.

If consciousness and the cosmos are one
then bodies glow with what warms them.
And as for the invisible side of love
better to leave that

for another time.
(A different light would make a different world.
A different world would perhaps make you
a little different.)

I who am only myself
a full answer to a question that has not been asked
unshakeable, irrevocable, nonetheless
look at you tenderly.

[MK]

Flyer's Fall

You tried out those great wings in flight.
But you were held to earth by a golden chain.
All your efforts appeared to be the height
of heroism. But weren't. (How could they be?) The sustain-

ing hope that one day you'd escape, be whirled
up to the azure, was but a cuirass,
thin, brazen, tossed away on some battlefield
of olden times. A compass

without a needle in a soldier's palm
as he succumbs, weak-kneed, to the sand
or to the steppe in a snow-storm;

a man found first and skinned
by the vultures, suffering as his warm
blood grows cold; aground.

[DR]

Après le Déluge

The immortal lips unwiped.
The sun transparent, a cognac bottle dropped

as soon as drained by an abandoned
god. The doves valiantly defend

what of the high places has survived disaster.
Here and there bits of plaster

come down on the heads of the mortals who'd let
raw nature overwhelm old habit.

A peacock walking through the water-spill,
opening wide a shit-bespattered tail.

At the taxi windows a line of whores
chewing gum, tooting the horns.

Jewels gleaming on the fingers of the dark.
The winds returning to their sack.

[DR]

Dialectic

The epic of change is not the sudden
violent overturn of the immutable.

It is the simple moves made by the immutable:
heaven's chessboard, or rather backgammon-table.

[DR]

Genesis

In the beginning was the beginning
It arose tremulous out of nothing –
from a thick-matted layer of darkness
with red stains, a bit like
the *topoi*, say, of Oedipus.

And then the Sphinx came along,
with diamond-studded wings
(before, of course, the unleashing
of the waters) – plotting and scheming
everything to come.

[RB & PN]

On the Sublime

The view from fifty is breathtaking.
Everything seen through a pleasingly nebulous
red, pink, blue (the thing is
not to take these clouds for carnations and lilies,
as they do who are less than painstaking).

The darkness sets in at a slightly higher
altitude, poured out by the Chimera with unstinting hand,
as a vulture harrows the liver
and you start at length to sense how the quotidian,
the eternal inexorably blend.

I find those heights take the breath away,
where nothing seems impossible;
as if some hand has quietly wiped away
that gray rock, and where ennui
takes on the bouquet of a ripening apple.

[DR]

Ballad of the Uncertain Lover

Your name on misty window panes I write,
and wait at stops where you have often waited:
no harm itself, but leaves harm unabated.

That ancient azure sound – profound perfume –
your radiant voice like angels' tears above!
I love you in the way Othellos love.

But where love warms me – leaves me mesmerized –
Iago's there, and makes me shake in fright.
Your iambs, I say: let them stay on ice.

A poem's such a slight and fragile bloom,
that nourished by the proper sorrow thrives:
but one short breath of anger and it dies.

[AC]

95

Allegro

Does life exist *before* death? Well, if so
it can't be this one, stacked with suffering.
The blind land where the one-eyed man is king,
through which there spreads a curious warm glow,

has hair-cracks in it, gaps through which pulsate,
right across space-time, rays from far suns beaming –
sounds never heard, faint perfumes beyond dreaming –
waves that won't burn, although they penetrate.

Yet that's not it. A kind of *elseness* slips
through in scarce inklings, managing to float
across and past the inner dark that grips

and limits us. And even though the pivot
balancing real and unreal scarcely tips,
the bitter lump loosens that blocked the throat.

[RB]

Interior Monologue of Stephanos Martzokis

I drink this beer all night, dark and bitter.
I'm trammelled in a shroud of dusky blue.
On the wall just one word – *Fate* – is written.
It never was restrained, this love for you:
if I were more romantic I might say
I loved you in a mad rhapsodic way.

And yet . . . I'm checked, and in the moon's control
('whose silver plectrum strums on silent strings').
Discouraging, that disc! The moon's a scale
that weighs me – finds me light and faltering.
I swear: each dawn and midnight on this reef
another shipwrecked feeling comes to grief.

The glaring light of day discovers me
quite lost at sea, drowning in delusion.
Rich chrysanthemums, acacia trees,
hibiscuses: they're in the past. Profusion
of perfumes my garden yields no more:
drained of colour, dry – all weeds and thorns.

Now it seems the day grows dark again.
So sinister! I cannot fathom why . . .
ah, fog and snow, hail and venal rain,
corrupt with silvery smears the limpid sky.
Within your clear and azure eyes immersed,
I feel my temples pulsing – soon to burst.

[AC]

The Second Coming

So cold that night will be! (The night before
will be, however, just as icy-keen.)
Clinging lichen, mosses, trailing weed
will cover us. The dark will wail and roar.

And countless thousands will attempt but fail
even to lift a single leaf that falls.
Others still, whom ravenous hunger gnaws,
will for a rotten apple sell their soul.

Then fearsome sirens will begin to howl;
the angels – upside down, transfixed with fright –
will plunge in parachutes towards the ground.

Crippled by their plight, and dizzy-white,
they'll be engulfed within that greedy whirl –
the swirling of the void that circles round.

[AC]

Portrait of a Lady

(Mantua School, c. 1480)

Her neck, slender, glimmers with jewels
which don't so much as hint at the cesspool

of the once powerful city state's imperium
(now prey to the appetites of a pudendum).

The locks (style of Mantegna)
a silver rope-ladder

leading to the depths of the abyss,
beyond the foliage of Paradise.

Her eyes, midnight suns,
dazzle bystanders sentenced

to lifelong deprivation.
Her teeth a sickle inflicting decimation

– of course, the arrows played their part –
on an army (those legs apart

must have been similarly magnificent).
Her bosom, divinely fragrant

as the firm Lucca hills
now turned to the Duke's hell.

[DR]

The Return

Exile is our earthly norm.
I know this when I watch the stars
closely. The flower in the vase
confirms our doom.

We'll not miss lily, daffodil,
or any balm that seemed to scent
this affliction, this banishment,
once we've become imperishable.

With lamp, candle, torch and spark,
light wore us down. But we'll relive
everything it deprived us of
when we breathe unending dark.

[RB & PN]

Now Down Here

Now it's gone quiet down here. All
is calm. In thick soot the devils are resting.
Some are clipping their nails. Others are testing
their memories of bygone days. Round as a ball,

a mauve serrated moon dives and fades
in the hot brimstone that's all but spent.
The flames have died down. Now and then
a dusky swarm flies out of pitch-smeared glades,

black angels singing (the dark pit jubilates,
chanting 'In Excelsis', *largo* or *andante*).
One sole remaining angel defecates
behind a surly bust of Dante.

[MK]

Villanelle

The kiss you gave us
withered Medusas.

Undecaying, it offers
me skies, stratospheres.

But I got turned back
by the heavenly wolf-pack.

[PN]

'Profane Love'

About you there's nothing of Giorgione's
'Sleeping Venus'. And that's precisely what awes me.
Your eyes (even though closed) are waves that gnaw
across aeons at the wild crags inside me.

Your warm hand that lies on the counterpane
is a tree's branch stretched over a cliff.
Your breast is of earth.
Your hair has no trace of heaven.

[RB & PN]

Theology

Let me try putting it another way:
let's not lay all the blame on the Creator.
They might have used a condom,
Laius and Jocasta.

And Theseus could never have left the black
sail flying by an oversight.
For years I've been haunted by the suspicion
that what he did was right.

[DR]

Cleanthes

Cleanthes Nikolaou. Born in Drama
with distant roots in Thesprotia.
Symbolist, with tendencies to *Weltschmerz*
and awareness of the futility of worldly things.
You might say he was incurably elegiac.
Maintaining his distance from eternity,
he explored the intervening emptiness
with depth-sounding iambs. Which inevitably
got snagged down at the bottom.

[PN]

Triantafyllos Moraitis

I left behind me ten collections of poetry,
five for the many and five for the few,
with god-given lines, that trace
the boundaries of zero.
The many did not read them,
the few did not understand them.
Still unread, and past understanding,
even though I do not live, I hope.

[PN]

Tryphon Deimezis

The one whom the crowds cheered
in air-conditioned auditoria, or in private,
who 'versified an otherworldly music
using the celestial chords of human destiny,'
who 'had already risen to heaven' (Nezeritis),
this cenotaph commemorates.

[PN]

Daniel Misrahis

Instead of my own epitaph I've engraved
– reciprocating from this final resting place –
the epigram the deathless Patroclus Yiatras
would have lavished upon me:
'Talentless. His only good poem
was the verse he did not write.'

[PN]

Constantine Barbes

Half-buried beneath his own immortality,
with his other half he conversed with death,
chattering incessantly, enunciating
objections scarcely convincing –
to be more precise: hastening the process of decay
by his portentous, ponderous tropes,
insults to any language.

[PN]

C. P. Triantis

Triumphant. Prince of poets
(for others, king of prose).
But also the essay's dedicated
curator, searching under the surface
of things. Above all: iconoclast.
He recited in a subdued voice, as befits
one who always rises
to the occasion. Wise is now
the very earth that covers him.

[PN]

Leonidas Kandarakis

Fate lavishly bestowed two times upon me,
one for life and one for art.
Carelessly, however, I wasted
both of them on the latter.

Now down here, where matters of poetry
scarcely apply, I spend my hours weaving baskets,
occasionally playing backgammon with Patroclus Yiatras.

[PN]

Stephanos Calcanes

Death carried him off by a slip of the pen
forgetting that he was immortal.
Wherefore
he perambulates perspiring around the slippery
banks of Cocytus along with fellow sufferers
protesting, night and day calling in aid
sonnets and odes and prizewinning compositions.

[DR]

Patroclus Yiatras

Here rots the – nonetheless unfortunate –
body of Patroclus Yiatras the cynic
(his spirit survives, I suppose, in these lines).
He wrote epitaphs for fellow poets – compositions
displaying a certain engagement.
I believe you may have felt, passer-by, that his
piteous pages, now lying open before you,
are not without some usefulness.

[PN & RB]

Einstein

Where are you going in that cloud of hair?
Your pure mind reached and held the perfect note
to counterpoint your animal desire,
leaving those terrified of dark in doubt.

You saw as one, infinity and nought
and chaos ('shady garden of the void')
blossomed forth resplendent in your thought
with wilderness and city unified.

Beyond *thisness* and *elseness, here* and *there*,
radiant and magnificent you rowed
into the universe's heart of dark

where no rain ever falls, or sleet or snow,
and time itself lies open everywhere,
a wide and waveless ocean, dense and black.

[RB & PN]

Cavafy

The multicoloured paper masks you donned
and year in, year out, changed afresh each day,
hid wrinkles, ironed their evidence away,
saved you from scorn within your demi-monde.

But only when you put by masks for good
did you see in the naked glass your face
and, meeting Time's eyes straight there, realize
that Time craves flesh, not John the Baptist's food.

But now your flesh is word, and your word's power,
nourished by Time, lays bare the human soul:
its majesties, its horrors, its decays.

And not just that. Your word lays bare the ways
that the soul is what a poem's lines reveal:
sucking the nipple, no mere pacifier.

[RB]

Byron

No, it was not the cries of slaves so strongly
moved you, nor thought of flesh hacked to the bone.
The reason you wound up in Missolonghi
was to be rid of nightmares of your own.

No hero you, but neither a pariah.
Your one desire to make love with your Muse.
How greatly, if you knew, it would amuse
you, now, to have become freedom's Messiah.

O noble bard, unquenchably Byronic,
who all-revered have won the highest praise,
unwilling heir to treasuries ironic,

I beg you as a favour. Please arise
from your immortal sleep, not in a daze,
and give me, too, a death like yours for prize.

[RMB]

T. S. Eliot

April isn't the cruellest month. When you died
in January, that was still harder to bear
when even the lilacs bled
and green was dressed in mourning everywhere.

For – since the Muses had wanted
you to become Tiresias (no disrespect
to Oedipus) – all you'd desired had been granted:
to connect nothing with nothing.

Among those other old men bound for death
with nothing left to hope for, or expect,
when your turn came to travel on the boat

you faced the far side, stood upright, erect,
(your woolly muffler wound around your throat)
and no obol tucked between your teeth.

[RB]

Borges

You saw things through your innards, for your eyes
were birth-blighted before you even blinked.
You fathomed depths beyond the boundaries
known to the sighted, long believed extinct.

Descending mazy tunnels underground
you wove your ways through hidden labyrinths
and far away from wastes and crowds you found
gardens where time's not passed in hours or months.

(In Rethymno you spoke of miracle,
of 'quiet breath suffusing hearts of storms',
holding your empty glass as if brimful.)

Living meanings, you plucked things' cores and forms –
leaf-veins, afternoon-hues – light's own strings,
while others caught no more than shades of things.

[RB]

George Seferis Among the Statues

You measured out your life with coffee spoons
looking out over sluggish city rivers
from behind your consulate's grey window
as evening fell upon the green
like a bird with broken wing.

You spoke about cool and shady agapanthi
but were awoken by the hum of time
among dark meadows where naked men
trembling in thick mist upon their knees
fumbled among asphodels.

In your time, nothingness was hidden
by nothing. The blackness leaked light.
But our nights are pockmarked with holes
that waft the stench of rubbish.
Cold ash

falls unseen from the ceiling.
It collects on the furniture. Doors creak
unlatched, while warm, well-fed and
sleek-haired on their balconies

the Euplocami Nychtemeri
discover that you are a Conservative
by confusing history with the meaning of history.
(They sweat in vain to twist your every line
as if to bend Odysseus's bow.)

Now you while away your death beneath a palm tree
breathing the black serenity of the dead.
surveying those who are arriving
rowing with broken oars.

[RB]

Epilogue

And surely there must be some final act,
some closing scene, or some defining gesture –
a single stroke so focused and exact
it serves alone to summarize the lecture.
Within the soul the fitful glowing ember,
dampened once, remains inert and black.

And then of course there will be final words;
not deathless last pronouncements of the great,
but ordinary things we've often heard:
'Good day!' 'Chin up!' 'Can't tell you, I regret . . .'
'Yes, give me one as well – a cigarette'
'This is not the place I'd have preferred'.

[AC]

Selected Prose Writings

Poetry and Reality

an extract

POETRY AND TIME, I

Poetry is the timeless present tense. For it strips the past and present of their temporality: it detemporalizes the images of the past by detaching them from memory; it erases the present's topical elements, immersing it in a virgin oblivion. In poetry, past and present meet at a non-temporal point, in a profound, indissoluble, perennial present.

POETRY AND READING

The experience of poetry does not terminate with its reading. This is the initial contact, our act of acquaintance with it. The experience of a poem is also the experience of its recollection, which is not the same as the experience of reading it. This is because our response is modified by new events in our life that have intervened. The experience of recollecting a poem is what might be termed covert reading, since each time we remember a poem, we invisibly re-read it. The reading of a poem never ends; it recontinues every time we come into covert contact with it. More: it continues even when the poem sleeps within us, in a constant state of gestation, interrupted by moments of actualization, by the moments of covert contact.

POETRY AND RHYTHM, I

The poem is rhythm embodied in lines and fleshed out with words. The line may be in prose. In other words, the line is not a matter of fixed form. It may be metrical, free, or in prose, depending upon the mood or requirements of the rhythm (in this last case, the line length is equal to what we feel to be the smallest unit of rhythm).

A poem starts out from a sense of rhythm that brings certain words to the surface. Or it may start out from a sense of certain words that brings a certain rhythm to the surface. Then the two proceed, in fusion.

POETRY AND PROGRESS

Poetry does not progress. Only its face changes. Or, if it *does* progress, we are in no position to know that. This is because poetry is not the poetic text itself but what we sense when we read a poetic text. We cannot compare the poetry of our own time with that of any other, because we cannot know what people of that other age experienced from the poems of their own time. What we term the poetry of another age actually means the poems of that time as we experience them now. In other words, it, too, is poetry of our time.

POETRY AND RHYTHM, II

The poetic experience is none other than the happy result of a clash of two rhythms: the rhythm of everyday life, which is the sense of the experience of 'current' time; and the rhythm of the desire to transcend this sense, which is the experience of the quest for poetic (that is, non-temporal) time. Each poetic experience diverts us from the dreary track of every-day life towards an ideal rhythm along a delightful side-path.

POETRY AND MORALITY

In the last analysis, a poet's morality is a question of linguistic behaviour. Any lack of morality in his poetry is not commensurate with the reprehensible things he may say, but with his inability to purge himself of the original sin of language: that is, of the fission of the word into signifier and signified. Poetic language is the language of a form of religion: of man's desire to elevate himself into the paradise of expression. Its morality depends upon the passion with which it repossesses the sign's lost unity.

POETRY AND TIME, II

Since it is by its nature psychological, the poetic condition is not something that can last. This is because duration means continuity, and continuity means succession, repetition, uniformity, stagnation; that is to say, exactly what the poetic condition seeks to subvert. The sense of internal harmony is a dynamic sense, not a static one. But it is a paradoxical sense in that it is statically dynamic, or rather, dynamically static. It is a dynamic sense because, when attained, it puts an end to the experience of time as succession, it suspends the taste of continuity, of monotony, of 'stasis' in time. Yet this suspension simultaneously entails another stasis (a momentary stasis, a *stillness*), which is dynamic precisely *because* it is momentary, not successive, 'temporal'.

POETRY AND EVERYDAY LIFE

The emotions and beliefs that a poet expresses in a poem are not identical to his emotions and beliefs in everyday life. For poetry is a condensed and exalted discourse, and the sustenance of things is more profound when it is in a poem than when it is outside it. This is the other reason for poetry's lack of duration. The poetic self is the self in its utmost form, and one cannot sustain the weight of this form for long. Poetry, the most human condition, is at the same time the most inhuman. The poetic experience is so highly charged that its prolongation might crush the person undergoing it. It is impossible to live constantly in the poetic state.

Everyday life is essential for one to enjoy poetry, just as poetry is essential to help one to endure everyday life.

POETRY AND HISTORY

The view that history advances through human antitheses, that its motivating force is the class struggle, is correct, but such a view embraces only the visible aspect of the matter. The more profound question is: why do the classes struggle among themselves? From the depths of this question, the answer sounds out serenely, splendidly, imperturbably: poetry is the motivating force of history. All the acts of history are dictated by humanity's desire to experience the ideal condition. The Marxist dream of a classless society, the vision of a blissful societal tranquillity, of a dynamic stasis, is none other than the transposition of the vision of the 'poetic condition' onto a collective level. But this vision, like that of the Platonic society, functions within the framework of temporal succession (which accumulates antitheses): being a 'temporal' vision it is thus forever unrealized. However, the Marxist vision is closer to poetic reality than the Platonic, because it is classless. Its harmony stems from an abrogation of human antitheses, which, like the harmony of poetry, is the product of the fusion of these antitheses, not – as in the Platonic vision – of their compromise.

POETRY AND REALITY

Poetry expresses reality. But what is reality? It is not, surely, everyday reality, which poetry never expresses, but simply utilizes in order to transcend it. Everyday reality is the perishable stuff, but poetry cannot make poems out of that alone. Poetry expresses *real* reality, which, though invisible, is diffuse and pulsates within everyday reality; poetry expresses the most profound of realities, which is none other than humanity's unceasing, ardent, eternal longing to transcend our everyday condition, to experience ideal reality.

Real reality is the imperishable human longing for poetry.

[CW]

Eight Positions on the Translation of Poetry

1

If 'a poem should not mean but be' as Archibald MacLeish writes, then poetry is an act of self-identification. The intent identifies with the means; and it is impossible to separate the word from its meaning, signifier from signified. Poetic language is the language before the Fall; the single, undivided, ideal language (language in its ideal form), free from any dualism between body and soul: a body of language whose soul is its own skin. Therefore, poetic language could be defined as the *non-translatable language*: non-translatable because it is an absolute language; and since translation is an operation in which linguistic relativity is a prerequisite, this activity can be carried out only when the relationship between the signifier and the signified is arbitrary.

2

The translation of poetry (if we could speak of translation in the context of poetry) is the transfer of a poetic body from one language to a poetic body that belongs in another. In this case, the separation between the signified and the signifier can hardly be conceived, even in conventional terms. In poetry, the signified differs from that in other types of discourse, because its very substance is intrinsically determined by the materiality of the sign. Any change in this 'materiality' (i.e. any attempt to translate the signs) entails corruption not merely of their particular substance (i.e. primarily of their emotive charge), but also of the entire fabric of poetic language. Therefore, what we have referred to as transfer in the translation of poetry is a process that can scarcely be considered as one of reconstruction.

Reconstruction means building a form anew with identical materials, whereas in the translation of poetry the materials are different simply because languages are different. The translation of poetry is therefore a re-creation, or rather, it is the creation by means of the materials in the translator's language of a new poetic body: one that corresponds to that of the original (since the two cannot be identical), and that has a comparable weight and tone.

3

If the translation of poetry is impossible, then the translation of poetry is a genuine art.

4

In translating poetry the original is the experience, and the process of translation is the poetic act.

5

A meaningful theory of influence cannot be formulated if it is not supported by a meaningful theory of translation, because influence between two poets who write in different languages necessitates translation. In the last resort, the things that influence a poet are not lines in the original language, but those of the original transported into the poet's own language. No poet can take a poetic image from a foreign poet unless that image is put into words first, unless a rhythm of one's own language has been instilled into it. Whether a poet will appropriate the lines of a foreign poem depends on how the lines of that poem sound within the fabric and rhythms of the poet's own language. This does not mean that foreign influence necessitates a written translation. Each influence depends on there being a translation, whether this takes place on paper or in the poet's mind.

(If the translation of poetry is an art, and if poetic influence requires translation, then such influence does not undermine originality. A foreign poet's text is raw material for a poet, just as is any other.)

6

Translation is the most meticulous way of reading. Translators are the best readers.

7

Some of the best Greek poems are translations. Some translations are among the best Greek poems.

8

A history of literature that excludes translations is an incomplete history. An anthology of poetry that does not include translations is an incomplete anthology.

[PN]

Cavafy's Poetry of Irony

No other Greek poet has been such a good critical reader of his own work as Cavafy. The phrase 'Cavafy is a poet of the future', which he spread eloquently to the wider public through the small coterie of his admirers, was clearly dictated less by vanity and more by an awareness that a time would come when his poetry, even though out of step with the poetical norms of his day, would one day be recognized as great, and not just within the narrow confines of modern Greek. Cavafy was aware that the poetic discourse he had forged with so much toil and craftsmanship through the careful blending of the various stylistic currents of the nineteenth century and those of the ancient Greek world would ultimately be accepted into the poetic canon in spite of its eccentricity and, indeed, would shape that canon more so than usually occurs when a particular oeuvre is added to it.

This is what comes to mind when one considers the international influence of Cavafy today. Extensive criticism and commentary on Cavafy's poetry is available in many languages. International symposia on his work are held in various countries. Studies bearing titles such as 'Auden and Cavafy', 'Ungaretti and Cavafy', 'Plato and Cavafy' are published in international journals. Cavafy's poetry provides themes for works of art by great painters and composers. His work is taught not only in university departments of Modern Greek studies, but also in comparative literature courses around the world.

Today the influence of Cavafy's poetry among both his Greek and non-Greek readers would seem to have become something of a phenomenon, especially when we recall that Cavafy belongs to the earlier part of the twentieth century and has been read uninterruptedly since then. Nor is he a poet who had fallen into oblivion and subsequently enjoyed a revival or rediscovery. When one looks into his reception by the Greek reading public, it seems that Cavafy has been treated very differently from his junior Angelos Sikelianos, for example. The latter, after a period of neglect, now seems to have regained his reputation as a poet, even though as one who represents an age now past. The fascination with Cavafy, however, from the time of his death in 1933 to the present, has steadily increased; and it would seem that he is read more now than at any time in the past, and also with the same immediacy as is usually reserved for a contemporary poet. The same could be also said of his influence among non-Greek speakers, particularly from the 1960s onwards when his poetry reached a much wider audience through publication in many of the major western languages: English in 1952 and 1961, German in 1953, French in 1958, Italian in 1961 and Spanish in 1964. So the poet who was at his most creative in the last years of the nineteenth century and the first years of the twentieth century is read today as if he were a poet of the late twentieth century.

Cavafy's influence on non-Greek literary production has only recently received the scholarly attention and systematic investigation that it deserves. What concerns us here is not Cavafy's reception by the wider reading public, for the sales of translations of Cavafy's writings speak for themselves. Rather, we need to look at the influence of Cavafy on non-Greek practitioners of the art of poetry, for it seems that this influence is far greater than one might at first imagine. To the best of my knowledge, no other poet of the twentieth century has directly inspired so many poets writing in other languages through his poetry. I hasten to emphasize this last word, since the poems inspired by Mayakovsky and Lorca – two figures who may perhaps claim as much popularity as Cavafy outside of the languages in which they originally wrote – invariably concern their deaths: Mayakovsky's suicide and Lorca's execution. Cavafy, by contrast, inspires his fellow poets not because of some extraordinary event in his life, but almost exclusively because of his poetry. Furthermore, depictions of the man by his fellow poets invariably take the poetry itself as their point of departure.

Cavafy created a new poetic language by using a prosaic, unemotional language, which was nevertheless capable of creating in the reader an emotion analogous to the emotion produced by 'poetic' language, that is, by a language that is sensuous, whether lyrical or 'dramatic'. Cavafy's poetry *is* dramatic, yet it differs from the poetry of other dramatic poets (Dante, for example, or Eliot or Seferis) in that its language lacks sensuousness. The difference, I believe, lies in Cavafy's far more dense use of dramatic and tragic elements; so dense, in fact, that I would venture to term it 'ironic'. Cavafy is the first poet who uses irony as a key mechanism for the production of poeticism. The unique dramatic and tragic irony in Cavafy is characterized by the systematic and highly refined depiction of the contradictions that exist between what *seems* and what *is*. This feature, which also serves to shape his verbal irony, is precisely what makes his language capable of eliciting poetic emotion, thereby rendering sensuous language superfluous. And it is precisely this ironic quality of Cavafy which demonstrates the uniqueness of his poetic voice – a voice that allows us to view his work as formulating an altogether new type of poetry, a special kind of dramatic poetic discourse, which, since its principal element is irony, we may term *ironic* poetry, in contradistinction to 'lyrical' forms of dramatic poetry.

It is not my intention here to exaggerate the importance of this identification of a new kind of poetry; yet the aim is to underline how Cavafy's poetic expression is so innovative that it creates the sense that his poetry has been composed in a wholly new 'style'. And this observation takes us back to a point I made earlier, namely, the absence of aging in Cavafy's poetry. Since every style is the product of a particular period, the literary or other artistic works of an earlier period inevitably bear the signs of their times, signs of aging, irrespective of their inherent vitality, or perhaps even in spite of it. But Cavafy's poetry gives the impression of having been forged in a new style, because it is written in an unrecognisable style. And this is so because, having assimilated elements from the various styles of the period (Romantic, Parnassian, Symbolist, Aestheticist), in his best poems Cavafy succeeded in blending all these elements into a wholly new poetic style, that likewise distanced itself from all these influencing elements. It is a style, also, that retains an independence from the various emerging modernist poetical precepts of the early twentieth century – which, however, while not unassociated with the spirit of the age, still open the way for a unique, highly personal poetic modernism. The uniqueness of this modernism is the product of Cavafy's use of irony. And, above all, this unique use of irony – which, as a basic element of the human condition, is constant through time – is seen to remove the usual hallmarks of style from the components of the Cavafian poetic amalgam and to forestall any tendency for it to erode with age.

I believe this is the reason why today Cavafy's poetry appears even stronger than before. As the period in which we live is one particularly marked by irony – and, for many, by indifference – the unbridled relativism of our times makes it difficult to draw a distinction between the real and the apparent. So Cavafy's ironical tone, with its ability to lay bare human self-deception, has become more timely than ever. Indeed, this tone has now been presented with the opportunity to reveal to the full the strength of its realism.

[JD]

Identity and Poetic Language

an extract

Perhaps one of the most paradoxical ideas that has gained currency in the last decades of the twentieth century, at least within the sphere of literary studies, is that of the 'Death of the Author'. According to this idea, which has become the stock concept of post-modern literary theories, the actual author of a literary work is not the person who happens to sit down and write it, but the writing itself (*écriture*), that is, the Language, to be exact (with a capital L) – the great transcendental force which created the world, which *is* the world, and outside which there is nothing. The person writing a literary work, so the theory goes, is a mere intermediary who executes the 'desire' of Language to incarnate its own transcendental, divine spirit in tangible (i.e. written) form; or, to put it more plainly, such a person is an intermediary who executes the desire of Language to make literature. And precisely because this spirit is transcendental, the person (who, by the act of writing, executes this literary desire of Language) loses his or her own voice, his or her own self, his or her own identity. This person, then, is transformed into a neutral 'hand cut off from any voice, borne by a pure gesture of inscription (and not of expression)', a hand that 'traces a field without origin', indeed, a field that 'has no origin other than in Language itself'.*

Language (again with a capital 'L') takes this 'hand' from the mass of people who speak it and write it as language (with a small 'l': *langue*). Its choice of agent is random. In this respect, Language differs from the older transcendental force, i.e. God, whom it has dethroned. The relationship of Language with the vehicle of its literary desire, with the

---

* See the note on page 146.

'scriptor', as we now apparently need to call the author, is not the same as the relationship that once linked God with His elect (Moses, for instance), whom He chose because He saw that this particular person possessed certain qualities that made him capable of conveying the Divine Will to humanity. This is because, in contrast with God, Language is not interested in people, whom it uses simply to assure itself of its transcendentality.

No less paradoxical would seem to be the manner in which this theory has been formulated and, to a significant extent, the manner in which it has been received, especially when we consider two facts. First, that the style of its proponents is anything but impersonal: by which I mean, theirs is a particularly expressive style, not to say a narcissistic one. And second, that some of the authors who claim that the author is dead are adulated as great authors precisely by those whom they themselves have convinced of the author's death.

Can it really be that literary writing is a field where we are expected to trace the absolute rule of an uncontrollable and despotic power, and one where every trace of the writer's individual identity, all attempt at expression, has been obliterated? Or is it possible that within this field there is a weak point that can be manipulated and utilized by the writer for his or her own expressive ends? [...]

Regardless of the extent to which language may have its own will, and however extensive may be that part of language which the poet is unable to control, the part that the poet *is* able to control is what actually moulds the part that is uncontrollable into poetic discourse. This part, the part of the language that *can* be moulded by the poet's expressive will, is formed by the nature of the poet's spoken discourse (*parole*). No poem is a real poem unless it possesses the character of the poet's spoken discourse. which is shaped by the poet's deeper self and which in turn shapes the voice in the poet's text. [...]

The poetic text is personal and, at the same time, impersonal discourse, though not in the sense of the transcendental impersonal attributed by the theories in question here. It is personal insofar as it could not have been created at all if the character of the poet's own oral language were not already present within it, as a kind of 'yeast', which has, so to speak, 'leavened' the poet's voice. On the other hand, the poetic text is impersonal insofar as the character of the poet's speech is not necessarily apparent within the poem. However, the poet's spoken discourse is latent, first, because poetic discourse itself imposes on the poet's voice not only the transcending of autobiography but also amplification – by a further element that is indispensable: the voice of the human community. And this is precisely what imbues the individual voice with the profoundest humanity. Second, to elaborate the baking analogy, the poet's speech is latent because oral language is the 'yeast' in the 'dough': that is, its character is precisely what has been deployed in transforming into poetic text the 'dough' of the poet's spoken discourse, which is also the language of the speech community to which the poet belongs. This character is, however, 'mixed into' the voice of the poetic text that the poet has created. Thus the individual voice of the poet continues to subsist within the text, as a presence, a breath, a spirit, which constantly checks and cancels out the *writtenness* of the poetic text. The discourse of a poetic text is oral: it is living discourse, relying on the form of writing to fuel its existence. [...]

The transformation of common linguistic 'dough' into poetic language, by means of the 'leavening' provided by the poet's personal oral idiom, is by no means 'borne by a pure gesture of inscription', but rather by the poet's own movement towards literary expression. And this movement is precisely what causes the leaven to consist of more than merely linguistic elements. For the movement is part of the leaven itself and no more or less than the poet's desire to articulate what he or she feels about the world and about being in it. If anything exists, then, 'outside' the text, it is this human desire to speak about the world, which far from being generated by language, is itself the generator *of* language. In poetry, this desire is led to the form – the highest form – of literary expression, and it is the achievement of this highest form that renders the poet a creator.

I should excuse myself, perhaps, for using the theoretically unfashionable terms 'expression' and 'creation', both of which are supposedly the exclusive property of the Romantics. But I believe that we need to describe the poetic phenomenon more accurately than can be done by deploying theories such as that of the 'Death of the Author'. The poet is more than a non-existent something. The poet is a creator. The poet creates an entity that has not existed prior to his or her act of creation; for before the poem itself there is no poetic language to be drawn on. Each word in a poem constitutes a new beginning, forming its own poetic nature out of nothing. Nor is a word's poetic quality transferable to any other poem, since it acquires its poetic substance from the particular words that surround it. A word's poetic substance (its *poeticality*) is created with and within the poem that contains it, and it exists only for and in that particular poem.

Of course, I use the word creator here with a small 'c', even if for the sake of greater lucidity I employ biblical images. I hope that these images are salient and meaningful, for poetic language is, after all, that of an irreducible *religiousness* insofar as it embodies the human need to be redeemed from the original sin of language: the fracture of the word into signifier and signified. Poetic language is the highest form of man's endeavour to rise to the paradise of expression. The success of poetic language depends equally on the extent to which it regains the lost unity of the sign and on the passion it brings to bear in doing so.

[JD & RB]

Notes

Field of Mars, p. 27 ff

In Greek, 'Pedion Areos', a park in Athens. See Introduction, p. 17.

Death in Exarchia, p. 31

A mainly residential neighbourhood in central Athens where Vayenas lives.

Death will come . . . , p. 32

The first three lines echo the first lines of one of Cesare Pavese's untitled final poems, written March 22, 1950. 'Verrà la morte e avrà i tuoi occhi / questa morte che ci accompagna / dal mattino alla sera . . . ' (Death will come and have your eyes / this death that accompanies us / from morning until evening . . .)

Biography, III, p. 39

Katerini: a town in central Macedonia, northern Greece.

Biography, VI, p. 41

The first line echoes 'For the New Year 1976', a poem by Richard Berengarten (Burns): 'December 31st 1975, head bunged up with the year's / unwritten and half-written poems . . . ' (*Inhabitable Space*, Groningen, 1976, p. 4).

Biography, IX, p. 42

Alexander Kerensky (1881–1970): last prime minister of the Russian Provisional Government prior to Lenin's election by the All-Russian Congress of Soviets. Lenin's arrival by train in St Petersburg in April 1917 precipitated the October Revolution six months later.

Biography, XVI, p. 44

Syntagma (Constitution) Square: in central Athens, fronted by the Greek Parliament.

The last line echoes a line in the same poem by Richard Berengarten (Burns) quoted in Biography, VI above: 'and so go forward into the last quarter of this century'.

Clean Curtains, p. 54

The opening line echoes that of 'Pavana Dolorosa' by Geoffrey Hill (*Tenebrae*, London, 1978, p.19).

Chagall's 'Man leaping over the city': an allusion to John Matthias's poem 'A Painter' (*Turns*, London, 1975, p. 56), which Vayenas translated and included in *Flyer's Fall*.

National Garden, p. 55

The title refers to the large public park in central Athens, formerly known as the Royal Garden, close to Syntagma Square and behind the Greek Parliament.

Calvos in Geneva, p. 57

Andreas Calvos (1792–1869) was a major nineteenth-century Greek poet. Born in Zakynthos, he settled with his father in Italy where he later met the Italian poet and revolutionary Ugo Foscolo (1778–1827). Also born in Zakynthos to a Greek mother, Foscolo became a mentor to Calvos, who served as the Italian poet's secretary and in 1816 followed him in exile to London, remaining in his service until 1817, when their friendship ended after a serious quarrel. Between 1821 and 1825, Calvos lived in Geneva, where his first volume of odes, *Lyre* (1824), was written and published.

The Italian poet and dramatist mentioned is Count Vittorio Alfieri (1749–1803).

Count Giovanni Capo d'Istria, known in Greece as Ioannis Kapodistrias (1776–1831), was born in Corfu. After serving in the diplomatic service of the Russian Tsar Alexander I, in 1827 he was elected the first head of state of independent Greece.

Line 12 alludes to the first stanza of Calvos's ode, *To Samos*: 'Freedom requires Virtue and Daring'.

Interior Monologue of Georgios Hortatzis, p. 60

Georgios Hortatzis (c. 1550–1660): Cretan dramatist and poet.

Pasiphaë: wife of King Minos of Crete, who mothered the Minotaur after conceiving a passion for a white bull.

The Perfect Order, p. 62

PAOK and Panathinaikos: Greek football teams, respectively from Thessaloniki and Athens.

Terzanides: a footballer.

Veria: town in northern Greece, near Thessaloniki.

Lord Byron in Rethymno, p. 65

Rethymno: town in Crete where Vayenas lived from 1980 to 1991. For further references, see 'Love Games', p. 66, 'Hymn (or Ode perhaps)', p. 70, 'Barbarous Odes, II', p. 77, and 'Borges', p. 118.

Jorge Luis Borges in University Street, p. 67

The only dated poem in Vayenas's oeuvre, written immediately after the poet's chance encounter with Borges in central Athens. This meeting led to the Argentinian author of *Labyrinths* receiving an honorary doctorate from the University of Crete in the following year.

The English writer G. K. Chesterton (1874–1936), greatly admired by Borges, was famous for his elegant and delicate walking sticks, as well as for writing about them.

Polyphemus: name of the Cyclops in Homer's *Odyssey*.

Dionysios Solomos (1798–1857) is considered to be Greece's national poet.

Dolce Stil Novo, p. 68

The title refers to the 'Sweet New Style': poetic movement in 13th-century Italy that emphasized love and reverence for female beauty. Its modes were derived from the Provençal troubadours. Developed by Dante, Cavalcanti and later, Petrarch.

Hymn (or Ode perhaps), p. 70

'Devotion': prose poem in Rimbaud's *Les Illuminations* (1880).

Philippoi: ancient city in Macedonia, founded by King Philip II, father of Alexander the Great.

The line quoted from Seferis occurs in *Mythistorema* (20): see *Collected Poems*, trans. Edmund Keeley and Philip Sherrard, London, 1982, p. 51.

Via degli Apuli: street in Rome.

Grevena: town in northern Greece.

Spinoza, p. 74

Baruch de Spinoza (1632–1677): Jewish Dutch philosopher of Portuguese Sephardic origin, who worked as a lens grinder. He died of a lung illness possibly caused by fine glass dust. 'Rosa Raczewski née Vamprotten' seems to be a fictional figure. Spinoza is thought to have been a model of celibate virtue.

Barbarous Odes, X, p. 79

Romos Filyras: poet (1898–1942). Following signs of mental disturbance, probably caused by venereal disease, in 1927 he was admitted to a psychiatric hospital, where he spent the rest of his life. Several references are made here to Filyras's poem 'Moon' (published in *To Trito Mati* [The Third Eye] 4–5, Athens, 1936), from which the epigraph is also taken.

Après le Déluge, p. 91

Title of a prose poem in Rimbaud's *Les Illuminations*.

On the Sublime, p. 94

The title alludes to the Greek writer Longinus's treatise on aesthetics and the uses of good writing.

The Chimera: in Greek mythology, a monstrous creature composed of parts of other animals.

Interior Monologue of Stephanos Martzokis, p. 97

Stephanos Martzokis: poet born on the Ionian island of Zakynthos (1855–1913). His first collection, *Ballades*, was published in 1889. See Introduction, p. 21.

The Second Coming, p. 98

The title echoes that of W. B. Yeats's poem of 1920.

Garland, p. 105 ff

The collection consists of epitaphs for fictional poets.

Cleanthes, p. 105

Drama: town in northern Greece, Vayenas's birthplace.

Thesprotia: prefecture in Epirus, facing the Ionian Islands and Italy.

Stephanos Calcanes, p. 112

Cocytus ('river of wailing'): one of the five rivers encircling Hades, the others being Acheron, Phlegethon, Lethe, and Styx.

Patroclus Yiatras, p. 113

A complex and ironic persona of the poet himself. The name of this putative composer of all the epitaphs in *Garland* is also that of the fictional Greek translator of *The Waste Land*, as encountered in the first of the three Borgesian fables that comprise Vayenas's 1976 prose book *I syntechnia* [The Guild]. On this *jeu d'esprit*, see the Introduction, p. 18, and the book by Grigoris Pentzikis listed in the Bibliography, p. 149.

T. S. Eliot, p. 117

This poem contains four references to *The Waste Land*. The first line contradicts its famous first line. The lilacs in line 3 recall Eliot's 'lilacs out of the dead land'. Tiresias appears in lines 218 and 228. The phrase 'to make nothing connect with nothing' echoes Eliot's: 'I can connect / Nothing with nothing'.

George Seferis Among the Statues, p. 119

This poem is a web of references, mainly to Seferis. For the first line, see T.S. Eliot, 'The Love Song of J. Alfred Prufrock', line 52.

Euplocami Nychtemeri: these creatures occur in singular form in Seferis's 1941 poem, 'Kerk Str. Ost, Pretoria, Transvaal', where the animal is identified as 'the silver pheasant of China . . . strutting idly about its cage' (*Collected Poems*, trans. Edmund Keeley and Philip Sherrard, London, 1982, p. 277).

Eight Positions on the Translation of Poetry, p. 130 ff

The dictum 'A poem should not mean but be' is taken from the last two lines in Archibald MacLeish's poem 'Ars Poetica', 1926.

Cavafy's Poetry of Irony, p. 133 ff

Vayenas's abridged version of the introduction to *Conversing with Cavafy: An Anthology of Foreign Cavafy-inspired Poems* (see Bibliography, p. 148).

From Identity and Poetic Language, p. 137 ff

Quotations in this text are from Roland Barthes's essay 'The Death of the Author', in *Image-Music-Text*, trans. Stephen Heath, New York, 1977.

A Select Bibliography

This bibliography excludes poems and essays by Nasos Vayenas published in journals, whether in Greek or other languages; critical texts edited by Nasos Vayenas; pamphlets and other ephemera; and interviews and issues of journals dedicated to the poet. For a comprehensive bibliography, see the book by Savvas Pavlou, listed at the end.

POETRY

Πεδίον Άρεως [Field of Mars]. Athens: Diogenis, 1974; Gnosi, 1982.

Βιογραφία [Biography]. Athens: Kedros, 1978.

Τα γόνατα της Ρωξάνης [Roxane's Knees]. Athens: Kedros, 1981.

Ο λαβύρινθος της σιωπής [The Labyrinth of Silence]. Athens: Kedros, 1982.

Περιπλάνηση ενός μη ταξιδιώτη [Travels of a Stay-at-Home]. Athens: Kedros, 1986.

Η πτώση του ιπτάμενου [Flyer's Fall]. Athens: Stigmi, 1989.

Βάρβαρες ωδές [Barbarous Odes]. Athens: Kedros, 1992.

Η πτώση του ιπτάμενου, β' [Flyer's Fall, II]. Athens: Parousia, 1997.

Σκοτεινές μπαλλάντες και άλλα ποιήματα [Dark Ballades and Other Poems]. Athens: Kedros, 2001.

Στέφανος [Garland]. Athens: Kedros, 2004.

Στή νήσο των Μακάρων [On the Isle of the Blest]. Athens: Kedros, 2010.

PROSE

Η συντεχνία [The Guild]. Athens: Kedros, 1976.

TRANSLATIONS AND EDITIONS

Edgar Allan Poe and Giuseppe Tomasi di Lampedusa, *Λίγεια* [Ligeia]. Co-translated with Jenny Mastoraki. Athens: Stigmi, 1996.

(Ed.) *Συνομιλώντας με τον Καβάφη: Ανθολογία ξένων καβαφο-γενών ποιημάτων* [Conversing with Cavafy: An Anthology of Foreign Cavafy-inspired Poems]. Thessaloniki: Kentro Ellinikis Glossas (Centre for the Greek Language), 2000.

Richard Burns (Berengarten), *Μαύρο φώς: Ποιήματα εις μνήμην Γιώργου Σεφέρη* [Black Light: Poems in Memory of George Seferis]. Co-translated with Ilias Layios. Athens: Typothito, 2005.

BOOKS OF ESSAYS

Ο ποιητής και ο χορευτής: Μια εξέταση της ποιητικής και της ποίησης του Σεφέρη [The Poet and the Dancer: A Study of the Poetics and Poetry of Seferis]. Athens: Kedros, 1979. Based on PhD for Cambridge University, 1979.

Η εσθήτα της θεάς: Σημειώσεις για την ποίηση και την κριτική [The Gown of the Goddess: Notes on Poetry and Criticism]. Athens: Stigmi, 1988.

Ποίηση και μετάφραση [Poetry and Translation]. Athens: Stigmi, 1989 [2nd expanded edition, 2004].

Η ειρωνική γλώσσα: Κριτικές μελετές για τη νεοελληνική γραμματεία [The Language of Irony: Critical Studies on Modern Greek Literature]. Athens: Stigmi, 1994.

Σημειώσεις από το τέλος του αιώνα [Notes from the End of the Century]. Athens: Kedros, 1999.

Μεταμοντερνισμός και λογοτεχνία [Postmodernism and Literature]. Athens: Polis, 2002.

Η παραμόρφωση του Καρυωτάκη [The Deformation of Karyotakis]. Athens: Indiktos, 2005.

BOOKS OF CRITICISM ON NASOS VAYENAS

Savvas Pavlou (ed.), *Για τον Βαγενά: Κριτικά κείμενα* [On Vayenas: Critical Texts]. Nicosia: Aigaion, 2001.

Morphia Malli, *Μοντερνισμός, μεταμοντερνισμός και περιφέρεια: Μελέτη της μεταφραστικής θεωρίας και πρακτικής του Νάσου Βαγενά* [Modernism, Postmodernism and Periphery: A Study of the Translation Theory and Practice of Nasos Vayenas]. Athens: Polis, 2002.

Theodosis Pylarinos (ed.), *Νάσος Βαγενάς: Μελετήματα* [Nasos Vayenas: Studies]. Athens: Vivliothiki Trapezas Attikis (Attica Bank Library), 2004.

Grigoris Pentzikis, *Πάτροκλος Γιατράς: Ένας ποιητικός ήρωας του Νάσου Βαγενά – οι δύο πόλοι ενός προσωπείου* [Patroclus Yiatras: A Poetic Hero of Nasos Vayenas – the Two Poles of a Persona]. Athens: Sokoli, 2005.

Dimitris Kosmopoulos, *Η πτήση του ιπτάμενου: Μια εισαγωγή στην ποίηση του Νάσου Βαγενά* [Flyer's Flight: An Introduction to the Poetry of Nasos Vayenas]. Athens: Indiktos, 2007.

BOOK-LENGTH TRANSLATIONS OF VAYENAS'S POETRY

ALBANIAN

Endjet e nje joudhëtari, trans. Faslli Haliti. Tirana: Globus R., 2001.

BULGARIAN

Orfei na gornata zemia, trans. Zdravka Mihailova. Sofia: Nov Zlatorog, 2002.

DUTCH

Biografie en andere gedichten, trans. Marko Fondse and Hero Hokwerda. Amsterdam: Het Griekse Eiland, 1990.

Barbaarse Oden, trans. Marko Fondse and Hero Hokwerda. Groningen: Styx Publications, 1997.

ENGLISH

Biography, trans. Richard Burns. Cambridge: Lobby Press, 1978.

Biography and Other Poems, trans. John Stathatos. London: Oxus Press, 1979.

GERMAN

Waderung eines Nicht-Reisenden, trans. Alexandra Rassidaki. Koln: Romiosini, 1997.

ITALIAN

Vagabondaggi di un non viaggiatore, trans. Caterina Carpinato. Milan: Crocetti Editore, 1997.

Ballate oscure e altre poesie, trans. Filippomaria Pontani. Milan: Crocetti Editore, 2006.
La luna nel pozzo: 27 poesie di Nasos Vaghenàs, trans. Oddone Longo and Massimo Peri. Turin: Genesi Editrice, 2008.

ROMANIAN

Rătăcirile unui necălător, trans. Victor Ivanovici. Bucharest: Editura Seara, 1998.
Ode barbare, trans. Valeriu Mardare. Bucharest: Editura Omonia, 2001.

SERBIAN

Barbarske Ode, trans. Ksenija Maricki Gadjanski and Ivan Gadjanski. Beograd: RAD, 2002.
Pad Letača, trans. Ksenija Maricki Gadjanski and Ivan Gadjanski. Beograd: Meridian, 2005.
Pesme, trans. Ksenija Maricki Gadjanski and Ivan Gadjanski. Brankovo Kolo: Sremski Karlovski, 2008.

BIBLIOGRAPHY

Savvas Pavlou, *Βιβλιογραφία Νάσου Βαγενά 1966–2008* [Bibliography of Nasos Vayenas 1966–2008]. Nicosia: Kentro Meleton Ieras Monis Kykkou (Research Centre of Kykkos Monastery), 2010.

The Poet and the Translators

NASOS VAYENAS was born in 1945 in Drama, in northern Greece. He studied literature at the universities of Athens (1963–1968), Rome (1968–1969), Essex (1972–73), and Cambridge (1974–1979), where he wrote *The Poet and the Dancer*, his PhD thesis on George Seferis (published in Greek in 1979). His first book of poems appeared in 1974 and since then he has published ten more collections, a book of imaginative prose, as well as several critical works, among them *The Language of Irony*, which was awarded the Greek National Prize for Criticism in 1995. His poetry has been translated into many languages and he is the recipient of major literary awards, including the Greek National Prize for Poetry (2005) for his collection *Garland*, the Attilio Bertolucci Poetry Prize (Italy, 2007), and the Branko Radičević Prize (Serbia, 2007). Since 1992, he has been Professor of Literary Theory and Criticism at the University of Athens, where he now lives.

* * *

RODERICK BEATON is the Koraes Professor of Modern Greek and Byzantine History, Language and Literature at King's College, London. His books include the award-winning biography *George Seferis: Waiting for the Angel* (2003) and the novel *Ariadne's Children* (1995). He has written widely on Greek literature and culture from the twelfth century to the present, and his published translations from Modern Greek include works by Embirikos, Seferis, Solomos, and the novel *Fool's Gold* by Maro Douka. His edition and translation of *A Levant Journal* by George Seferis was awarded the Hellenic Foundation for Culture Prize for Translation in 2008. He is currently working on a monograph provisionally entitled, *Byron's War: The Greek Revolution and the English Romantic Imagination*.

RICHARD BERENGARTEN (formerly BURNS) is author of *The Easter Rising 1967* (1969), *Avebury* (1971), *Black Light: Poems in memory of George Seferis* (1983), *In a Time of Drought* (2005), *The Blue Butterfly* (2006), *Under Balkan Light* (2008), and other books of poetry. He has received the Eric Gregory Award, Keats Memorial Poetry Prize, Duncan Lawrie Prize, Wingate-Jewish Quarterly Prize, International Morava Charter prize and the Veliki Školski Čas award (Serbia). His poetry has been translated into more than 80 languages. His co-translation with Peter Mansfield of Antonis Samarakis's *The Flaw* appeared in 1969–70. In the 1970s, he founded the international Cambridge Poetry Festival. He is a Bye-Fellow at Downing College and a Praeceptor at Corpus Christi College, Cambridge.

JOHN CHIOLES has written widely on the modern performance of ancient tragedies, culminating in his work *Aeschylus: Mythic Theatre, Political Voice* (1995). He is currently working on a book on Sophocles. His Greek publications include: *Theoria tis Logotechnias* [Theory of Literature] (1995) and *Theoria tis Theatrikis Praxis* [Theory of Theatrical Practice] (2005) as well as a collection of short stories, *O Romeos to Prezoni ke i Ioulieta to Kleftroni* [Romeo the Pothead and Juliet the Snitch] (2004). As a theatre director he has staged many dramas, ancient and modern, including English and American plays. He is Professor of Comparative Literature at New York University.

ROBERT CRIST was educated at Haverford College and the University of Chicago, and has taught at several universities in the USA and in Greece, where he was a Professor at the University of Athens until 2004. He has written articles and books on Walt Whitman, William Faulkner and modernist poetry. His translations include works by Aris Alexandrou, Despina Lala-Crist, Nikos Kyriazis (pen-name Nicholas Snow), Constantine J. Vamvacas and, most recently, *The Complete Works* of Giorgos Heimonas. He is co-author with Ray H. Crist of *Listening to Nature: My Century in Science – A Memoir* (2004) and editor of *Grind the Big Tooth: A Collection of Contemporary Greek Poetry* (1998).

ALAN CROSIER has a PhD in philosophy as well as degrees in psychology, and is a freelance editor and independent scholar. He spends most of his time in Australia, but travels frequently, especially in China. Mallarmé and Valéry, along with other French poets, are at the centre of his efforts in poetic translation. He also works comfortably with many other languages, especially Italian and Spanish. He has been a lecturer in philosophy at Charles Sturt University and at Monash University.

JOHN C. DAVIS is a translator and Byzantinist who has lived and worked in Athens for the past 25 years. Following studies at St Andrews University and King's College, he completed his PhD at the University of Ioannina, on a late-Byzantine 'metaphrase' of Niketas Choniates's *History* (2004). His translations include unfinished poems by C. P. Cavafy (*Conjunctions*, 31, 1998) and Nikos Panagiotakes's study, *El Greco – The Cretan Years* (2009). His translation (with Athanasios Angelou) of the lament on the fall of Constantinople to the Crusaders by Nicetas Choniates was set to music by John Tavener and performed at the 1998 Byzantine Festival in London.

KIMON FRIAR (1911–1993) was a prolific translator of modern Greek poetry, notably of Miltos Sahtouris, Odysseus Elytis, Takis Sinopoulos, Yannis Ritsos and Manolis Anagnostakis. His best known translation is of Nikos Kazantzakis's *The Odyssey: A Modern Sequel* (1958). He edited the anthologies *Modern Poetry: American and British* (with John Malcolm Brinnin, 1951) and *Modern Greek Poetry: from Cavafy to Elytis* (1973), as well as two journals devoted to Greek culture, *The Charioteer* (1960–1962) and *Greek Heritage* (1963–1965). Born to an American father and a Greek mother in Imrali, Turkey, Friar studied and lived in the US, teaching at various colleges and universities there, before eventually settling in Athens. In 1978, he received the Greek World Award.

MARGARET KOFOD was born in Sydney, Australia. She studied piano in The Hague and later completed a degree in Modern Greek in Groningen, studying translation with Hero Hokwerda, who has translated a large body of Modern Greek literature into Dutch (including work by Nasos Vayenas). In 2000 and 2003, Margaret Kofod translated poems by Nasos Vayenas and Giorgis Pavlopoulos for Poetry International Rotterdam. In 2004 she moved back to Australia, where she now works as a piano teacher and as a translator from Dutch and Greek into English.

PASCHALIS NIKOLAOU completed his PhD at the University of East Anglia, and currently teaches literary translation at the Ionian University (Corfu). Articles on aspects of translation studies and especially on the relationships between translation and literary creativity have appeared in journals and edited volumes, as well as reviews, translations and poems in *The London Magazine*, *Modern Poetry in Translation* and *The Wolf*, among others. He is the co-editor of *Translating Selves: Experience and Identity between Languages and Literatures* (with Maria-Venetia Kyritsi, 2008), and reviews editor of the translation journal *mTm*.

DAVID RICKS is Professor of Modern Greek and Comparative Literature at King's College, London. His books include *The Shade of Homer* (1989) and *Modern Greek Writing: An Anthology in English Translation* (2003), and he has written essays on many Greek poets. His translations have appeared in various magazines and anthologies; his poems (some of which have been translated by Nasos Vayenas) in journals such as *Poetry* (and its ninetieth-anniversary anthology), *New England Review*, and *Southwest Review*.

JOHN STATHATOS is a poet, writer and photographer, born in Athens in 1947. Following studies in philosophy and political science at LSE, he became a freelance foreign correspondent, translator and independent publisher (Oxus Press), bringing several Greek poets to the attention of an English-speaking audience. He was based in London until 2002, and now lives in the island of Kythera, where he established the annual Kythera Photographic Encounters. His publications include *Image and Icon: The New Greek Photography* (1997); *A Vindication of Tlön: Photography and the Fantastic* (2001); *Fotofraktis: The Photographs of Andreas Embirikos* (2004) and *airs, waters, places* (2009). Profile: www.stathatos.net.

CHRIS WILLIAMS has published numerous translations of Greek poetry, including *A Greek Anthology: Poetry from the Seventies Generation* (1991). His doctorate is a comparative study of George Seferis and T. S. Eliot. More recently he has explored those aspects of Greek history and music which intersect with other traditions, in particular those of Turkey and the Jewish Diaspora. As founder member of the music group Troia Nova he contributed research material and original music to the BBC Turkish World Service series, *İki kere yabancı* (Twice a Stranger). The series dealt with the 1920s population exchange between Greece and Turkey and won the Sedat Simavi prize in 2004. He lives in London.

Acknowledgements

THE EDITORS wish to express their warm gratitude to the Alexander S. Onassis Foundation for the generous funding that has made this collaborative book possible. For critical readings of drafts, comments on particular translations, linguistic clarifications, factual information, or general encouragement and support, thanks are due to Josephine Balmer, Roderick Beaton, Catherine Byfield, Margaret Kofod, David Ricks, Melanie Rein, Aishwarya Subramanyam and Chris Williams; as well as to Panagiotis Michailidis for his assistance in preparing the manuscript. Special thanks are due to Peter Jay at Anvil Press, for his consistent belief in this project from its inception to its conclusion, and for his advice and support on many practical matters throughout the processes of compilation and editing. Likewise, to Kit Yee Wong at Anvil. Above all, the editors wish to record their appreciation of the invaluable help given by Nasos Vayenas in response to queries as well as for comments on the final typescript.

Many of the translations included in this volume are reprinted from literary magazines and anthologies of Greek poetry, sometimes in slightly variant versions. For the republication of these translations, acknowledgements are due to the following translators, along with their editors and publishers:

RICHARD BERENGARTEN (BURNS) for 'Eden' in MenCard series (London: The Menard Press, 1977); for extracts from 'Biography' in *Biography* (Cambridge: Lobby Press Editions, 1978), and 'Biography: the Poetry of Nasos Vayenas', *Journal of the Hellenic Diaspora*, VII (1), Spring 1980; 'Biography, II', *International Literary Quarterly* (www.interlitq.org), 12, Autumn 2010; and 'Cavafy', *Modern Poetry in Translation*, Third Series, 14, Autumn 2010.

RICHARD BERENGARTEN and PASCHALIS NIKOLAOU for 'Torment', 'Roxane's Knees', 'Barbarous Odes, XV', *Modern Poetry in Translation*, Third Series, 14, Autumn 2010; 'Interior

Monologue of Georgios Hortatzis', 'Dolce Stil Novo', 'Barbarous Odes, VII', *International Literary Quarterly* (www.interlitq.org), 12, Autumn 2010; 'Jorge Luis Borges in University Street', *Parnassus*, 32 (1 & 2), Autumn 2010.

JOHN CHIOLES for 'The Birth of Aphrodite' in *A Century of Greek Poetry 1900–2000*, ed. Peter Bien, Peter Constantine, Edmund Keeley and Karen Van Dyck (River Vale, NJ: Cosmos Publishing, 2004).

ROBERT CRIST for 'Barbarous Odes, XXIII' in *Grind the Big Tooth: A Collection of Contemporary Greek Poetry*, ed. and trans. Robert Crist (Pittsburgh: Sterling House, 1998).

KIMON FRIAR Special thanks to Attica Tradition Educational Foundation for permission to use Kimon Friar's translations: 'Apologia' and 'A Game of Chess', *Mews*, 1, April 1975 (Cambridge University English Society); 'Death will come . . .', *Poetry Wales*, 11 (3), Winter 1976; and 'Episode', *International Portland Review*, 3, 1982.

MARGARET KOFOD for 'The Performance', 'The Performance, II', 'Death in Exarchia', 'Ode', 'The Perfect Order', 'Spinoza', 'Barbarous Odes' nos. X, XIII, XVIII, XXVI and 'Omaggio a Dante' (retitled 'Now Down Here') in *Nasos Vayenas* (Rotterdam: 31st Poetry International Festival, 2000).

PASCHALIS NIKOLAOU for 'Eight Positions on the Translation of Poetry', *In Other Words*, 24, Winter 2004/5; 'Clean Curtains' and 'Kleanthis' (retitled 'Cleanthes'), *The Wolf*, 14, Spring 2007; 'Triantafyllos Moraitis', *Modern Poetry in Translation*, Third Series, 14, Autumn 2010; 'Daniel Misrahis', *International Literary Quarterly* (www.interlitq.org), 12, Autumn 2010.

PASCHALIS NIKOLAOU and RICHARD BERENGARTEN for 'Sostenuto' in *World Poetry Almanac 2009*, ed. Hadaa Sendoo; and 'Patroclus Yiatras', *International Literary Quarterly* (www.interlitq.org), 12, Autumn 2010.

DAVID RICKS for 'Barbarous Odes, II', *The London Magazine*, 36 (1–2), April/May 1996; 'Flyer's Fall', 'Après le Déluge' and 'Dialectic', *Modern Poetry in Translation*, New Series, 13, 1998; 'On the Sublime' and 'Theology' in *The Greek Poets: Homer to the Present*, ed. Peter Constantine, Rachel Hadas, Edmund Keeley and Karen Van Dyck (New York: W. W. Norton, 2010).

JOHN STATHATOS for 'Saturday', *Zenos*, 5, 1978, and in *Biography and Other Poems*, ed. and trans. John Stathatos (London: Oxus Press, 1979); and 'Orpheus in the Overworld', *2 Plus 2*, Fall/Winter 1984.

CHRIS WILLIAMS for 'Beautiful Summer Morning', *The Literary Review*, 25, 1980; 'National Garden', 'Calvos in Geneva', *The London Magazine*, 33 (6), August/September 1993; and 'Poetry and Reality', *The London Magazine*, 36 (1–2), April/May 1996.

Several of the above translations have also been published or republished in the following anthologies. Translators are given in brackets:

Dinos Siotis and John Chioles (eds.), *Twenty Contemporary Greek Poets* (San Francisco: Wire Press, 1979): 'Saturday' (John Stathatos).

Kimon Friar (ed. and trans.), *Contemporary Greek Poetry* (Athens: Greek Ministry of Culture, 1985): 'Apologia', 'Death will come . . .' and 'A Game of Chess' (Kimon Friar).

Chris Williams (ed. and trans.), *A Greek Anthology: Poetry from the Seventies Generation* (Peterborough: Spectacular Diseases, 1991): 'Beautiful Summer Morning', 'National Garden' and 'Calvos in Geneva' (Chris Williams).

David Ricks (ed.), *Modern Greek Writing: An Anthology in English Translation* (London: Peter Owen, 2000): 'A Game of Chess' (Kimon Friar); 'Flyer's Fall', 'Après le Déluge' and 'Dialectic' (David Ricks); 'National Garden' and 'Calvos in Geneva' (Chris Williams).

Peter Bien, Peter Constantine, Edmund Keeley and Karen Van Dyck (eds.), *A Century of Greek Poetry 1900–2000* (River Vale, NJ: Cosmos Publishing, 2004): 'The Birth of Aphrodite' (John Chioles); 'Apologia' and 'A Game of Chess' (Kimon Friar); 'Spinoza' (Margaret Kofod); 'Flyer's Fall' and 'Après le Déluge' (David Ricks).

Peter Constantine, Rachel Hadas, Edmund Keeley and Karen Van Dyck (eds.), *The Greek Poets: Homer to the Present* (New York: W. W. Norton, 2010): 'The Birth of Aphrodite' (John Chioles); 'Spinoza' (Margaret Kofod); 'Après le Déluge', 'Theology', 'Barbarous Odes, II' and 'On the Sublime' (David Ricks).